The Vested Interests

The Collected Works of Thorstein Veblen
(The Transaction Series)

Absentee Ownership

The Engineers and the Price System

Essays in Our Changing Order

The Higher Learning in America

Imperial Germany and the Industrial Revolution

*The Instinct of Workmanship and
the State of the Industrial Arts*

The Nature of Peace

The Place of Science in Modern Civilization

The Theory of Business Enterprise

The Theory of the Leisure Class

The Vested Interests

The Vested Interests

Thorstein Veblen

With a new introduction by
Irving Louis Horowitz

Routledge
Taylor & Francis Group

LONDON AND NEW YORK

Originally published in 1919 by B.W. Huebsch, Inc.

Published 2002 by Transaction Publishers

Published 2017 by Routledge
2 Park Square, Milton Park, Abingdon, Oxon OX14 4RN
711 Third Avenue, New York, NY 10017, USA

Routledge is an imprint of the Taylor & Francis Group, an informa business

New material this edition copyright © 2002 by Taylor & Francis.

Library of Congress Catalog Number: 2001041590

Library of Congress Cataloging-in-Publication Data

Veblen, Thorstein, 1857-1929.
    The vested interests / Thorstein Veblen ; with a new introduction by
    Irving L. Horowitz.
        p. cm.
    Originally published: The vested interests and the state of the industrial
    arts. New York: B.W. Huebsch, 1919.
    ISBN 0-7658-0865-X (pbk. : alk. paper)
    1. Industry. 2. Business. I. Horowitz, Irving Louis. II. Title.

    HD2326 .V4 2001
    330.1—dc21   2001041590

ISBN 13: 978-0-7658-0865-3 (pbk)

Contents

Transaction Introduction vii

Preface xv

1 The Instability of Knowledge and Belief 1

2 The Stability of Law and Custom 13

3 The State of the Industrial Arts 25

4 Free Income 45

5 The Vested Interests 61

6 The Divine Right of Nations 81

7 Live and Let Live 97

8 The Vested Interests and the Common Man 111

Transaction Introduction

Thorstein Veblen's Last Hurrah: Kept Classes, Vested Interests, and Common Men

It is nearly a century since Thorstein Veblen's classic texts on a full range of topics—from higher education to the industrial order, with stops along the way on the economics of war and the sociology of consumption—have appeared. We now accept him as the premier figure in twentieth-century American social thought. This has come about begrudgingly, since there is a widespread awareness that Veblen's analyses can be faulted on empirical and theoretical grounds alike. His thinly disguised moral posture was hardly calculated to make friends and influence economists. The magic of Veblen, that on which his reputation largely rests, derives not from being right on every prediction, but on his remarkable capacity to direct our collective attention to issues that matter. This ability to examine in a fresh way that which ails American society is well illustrated in his briefer pieces of *The Vested Interests*. If it can be said that Alexis deTocqueville showed us the bright side of early nineteenth-century pre-Civil War America, then it is with equal passion that Veblen revealed the dark side of that same society as its base shifted from an agrarian to an industrial system. The reader of these essays should be under no illusions: Veblen is a severe critic of the society he celebrated. In that paradox, one discovers the good heart of his social science darkness.

Thorstein Veblen has become an iconic figure. This is especially the case with institutional economists who would like to be sociologists, and sociologists who would like to think that they are not thoroughly ignorant of things economic. He is, in short, an intellectually accessible figure, if a somewhat marginalized one, in professional and occupational terms. The minus of this adoration is that criticism is not something that Veblen has had much of these days. And nothing is more deadly than hagiography disguised as evaluation or biography. Opponents ignore him with the same dedication as proponents adore him. One bracing aspect of *The Vested Interests* is that in these briefer pieces of which the work is composed, written for the literary crowd, Veblen comes through, warts and all. To ignore the warts is to pay scant attention to the achievement of the work as such.

Veblen is the sort of protean figure who derives his reputation from a curious admixture of brilliant global insights, generalizations that call us back to first principles, and personal asides that make us smile—but probably made his contemporaries more than a little angry with the object of his derision. He was not given to academic protocol, and I suspect that the strange group that now consider themselves Veblenians often do so for stylistic reasons. For to approach Veblen as a grand systems designer would be not only a waste, but a cruel joke on Veblen himself. The thin line between intellectual creativity and literary license, a line that Veblen criss-crossed with careless abandon on more than one occasion, gives us pause to consider whether it is scientific rigor or novelistic *aperçu* that make someone memorable. My approach to *The Vested Interests* is to take at face value the arguments he presents—meaning empirical value—and see how it is that a figure of such contrariness as well as contradictions survives in our minds while lesser figures of a more earnest sort pass into the dustbin of intellectual history.

Thorstein Veblen is the great American example of an academic social scientist who was also a writer turned prophet. Nowhere is this better on display than in *The Vested Interests*. He wrote eleven books (several of them, in particular *The Vested Interests*, derived from essays). Many of the chapters of these books first appeared as random essays in popular journals aimed at a literate, bourgeois audience of the college-educated and the business-trained—in short, the very people for whom Veblen exhibited little compassion, and some might say, the least appreciation. Indeed, over the course of the century, Veblen seems to have been transmuted from an economist to a sociologist. As economics veered to quantitative analysis of partial systems, and sociology took up the claims of qualitative analysis of whole civilizations, discussing Veblen in relation to American sociology from Giddings to Park seems far more sensible than any other option in the history of ideas.

The Vested Interests is the perfect indicator of these contradictory trends in the work and thought of Thorstein Veblen. He was radical in input, conservative in outcome; analytical in design, ideological in rhetoric; materialist in economic analysis, idealistic in his emphasis on law and custom as regulatory mechanisms of the management of society. Veblen was a socialist in his hopes for a business civilization, and a feudalist, to the point of being medieval, in his faith in industry, thrift, and integrity. These contradictions are inherent even in the title. The book is sometimes titled The Vested Interests and the State of the Industrial Arts—a rather clumsy title disguising in perfect Veblenian terms a life-long concern over the quality of work and the workplace. But the alternate title, The Vested Interests and the Common Man, speaks for his late-blooming concern with the fate of blue-collar America. In short, Veblen offers his classic pose on social status, intertwined with a growing interest in economic class—or better yet, the political prospects of that class.

In this sense, Veblen's work, although following the close of World War One, does not so much reflect what Eric Hobsbawm refers to as the "short" twentieth century lasting from 1914 to 1989 (the fall of Communism) as it does the last hurrah of the nineteenth century spilling over into the twentieth century. His is a specifically radical voice in a world in which issues of gender barely rise above a whisper and in which those of race rise not at all. That so many readers of Veblen continue to be charmed by his rhetoric is as much a function of his quaint sense of what matters as is any cutting edge sensibility of the postwar world coming to grips with American problems as world problems. Indeed, one is hard put to find in Veblen a sense of the global context in which America was operating in the early 1920s. His world remained from start to finish a nineteenth-century world. The Great War was a "disturbance," and issues of national self-determination were derided as "the self-aggrandizement of each and several at the cost of the rest." Isolationism was the operative principle—the conservative principle—of this radical son of the Midwest. The world became an "incursion of ideas and considerations that are alien to the established liberal principles of human intercourse." The League of Nations, then very much on the postwar table, became for Veblen "a blurred afterimage of the divine right of kings." Veblen ended his panegyric with an observation that such efforts at international order disguised "national pretensions, wrangles, dominion, aggrandizement, chicanery, and ill-will." It was the new format for "the old familiar trading stock of the diplomatic brokers who do business in dynastic force and fraud, also called *Realpolitik.*" While one may be somewhat embarrassed by the severity of Veblen's isolationism, the fact is that the League of Nations did little to preserve the peace and much to defend the commercial right of particular vested interests.

One argument Veblen adduces against prospects for some general interest to contain the "special interests" is the argument concerning the need for tariffs to support a national economy. For Veblen and "all adult persons of sound mind," the tariff is part and parcel of the price system itself, and hence the use of tariffs obstructs the growth of industry itself. No free marketer could have spoken with greater ferocity against the sabotage and the pettifogging special pleaders than this dedicated champion of socialism could! Consider Veblen's categorical assault on the idea of ethnicity, or at least small nationhood. Those Czechs, Slovaks, Slovenes, Ruthenians, Ukrainians, Croats, Poles and "Polaks," those "miniscule Machiavellians" clamoring for "national establishments"—whose sole real object in nation-building has no meaning in a time of peace—working at cross purposes with other mini-states. These are hardly the conventional arguments of the conventional Left. He could not care less for nationalism or self-determination. For Veblen, nations organized for "collective offense and defense in peace and war" are entities quite at odds with social organizations created to advance a "supposed community race—essentially based on sympathies and sentiments of self-complacency within itself." We have, in short, a man given to simplistic homilies like "Live and Let Live" as an answer to the driving forces of the twentieth century.

But if Veblen's late essays were reducible to a series of dialectical polarities, then his continuing reputation as one of the great figures of the twentieth century would long ago have gone up in a puff of smoke. One reads Veblen as a social scientific *gestalt*—a panoramic vision of the industrial genesis of modernism corrupted by its moral blindness. We are at home with these contrasts, and so we can enjoy his essays written for *Dial* magazine in 1918 and 1919 and refined somewhat for academic presentation as a set of lectures at Amherst College in the same period.

Veblen himself was unsure of the title. He calls it at first *The Vested Interests and the State of the Industrial Arts*. Later it becomes *The Vested Interests and the Common Man*. And to confuse matters further, it is given a wholly different title in parentheses: *The Modern Point of View and the New Order*. I am taking the liberty of calling this slender volume of essays simply *The Vested Interests*. Veblen himself offers the best reason for such an abbreviation. In the chapter entitled "The Vested Interests," he claims that "[a]ll that industry which comes in under the dominant machine technology, that is to say all that fairly belongs in the new order of industry, is now governed by business men for business ends, in what is to be done and what is to be left undone" (p. 99). That phrase encapsulates Veblen's harsh empirical view of the vested interests combined with a moral disapproval of the artificial limits this class sets on civilization and its thirst for progress.

But such a vision was old hat, even in the 1920s. The decade between 1910 and 1920 witnessed the emergence of a native socialism of some moral force no less than electoral power in the form of Eugene Victor Debs. Veblen reflected this in his final essay for *The Vested Interests*, "The Common Man." The ruling classes are pilloried as a set of "kept classes" who have better circumstances but not better values, and the place of the ruling classes is simply "to consume the net product of the country's industry over cost and so prevent a glut of the market." They also give rise to a series of intermediary classes, "such as the clergy, the military, the courts, police, and legal professions and occupations." These "subsidiary and dependent vested interests" are more refracted than reflective. They survive and even thrive on the "good will" of the controlling vested interests. "By sentiment and habitual outlook they belong with the kept classes." Of course, this was a disturbing wrinkle in the moral purity of Veblen's argument. It rated the academy—that most despised entity that also carried the message of rebellion and revolt—as little more than a vassal of the ruling class. How it came about that this particular subset of the ruling class (of which Veblen himself was a part) often gave voice to and articulated the needs of the "common man" was a task later taken up by sociologists of knowledge like Karl Mannheim and social psychologists like C. Wright Mills. Veblen had little time or patience with giving the intermediary classes a role other than that of lapdog. In this, he was very much a child of the Marxian revolutionaries.

Veblen knew that his formulation served as a crude, reductionist reminder of why he was being listened to in the first place. Though infrequent, the common man does makes an appearance on his own terms—not as a stepchild of the ruling classes, but as a class in its own right. It is true that the trade union movement, dominated by the American Federation of Labor (AFL), was not aware of the brewing divisions in labor's ranks that led to the birth of the militant Congress of Industrial Organizations that was organized on an industry-wide rather than craft basis. Veblen had a model in opposition to the AFL, namely, the International Workers of the World (IWW). Veblen saw the working class as the vanguard of revolutionary action. Independent farmers were hardly to be counted upon as friends of the organized worker, and the intellectual or professional elites were too busily engaged with their own to worry about tradesmen.

That left the proletariat as the only class willing to fight for something more that "something for nothing." Veblen refers to a "cleavage" brought about in the new order in business and industry. It turned out that a larger (95%) group, suspiciously like Karl Marx's proletariat was waiting in the wings to restore a vibrant capitalism, or at least its moral equivalent—a society of trade unionists who had nothing to lose but their assembly line. Veblen saw the "common man" in broad blue-collar terms: "somewhat irresponsible and unsteady in his aims and conduct." In the eyes of the guardians of law and order, he was "an undesirable citizen." The way into a glorious future, for Veblen, was to convert this "lack of respect and affection of the vested interests" into advanced forms of trade unionism. The wobblies of the International Workers of the World were to become the model for "the new order."

What evidence such syndicalism displayed in the past that can serve as a prototype for a new higher blue-collar morality is not made clear by Veblen—any more than it was made clear by Sorel in France. The idea of class collaboration was anathema to both advocates of syndicalism as a new morality, and not just a new way to gain better wages, hours and health conditions. What Veblen saw as the "modern era" was little more than a capitalism that was unreconstructed and unbridled. Non-economic issues such as psychological modes of increasing awareness of common goals between the vested interests and the working masses were never entertained by Veblen, even if the work of Elton Mayo and Frederick Roethlisberger was already well underway. In this, Veblen was part and parcel of the socialist as well as syndicalist tradition. The idea of vanguard parties, dictatorship of the proletariat, and generally authoritarian modes of behavior were anathema to Veblen. Hence, at the end of the day, Veblen was left with a dilemma: an economic order that was unpalatable and unacceptable at the political level—an order coming into being unknown to him. The conservative moralist as revolutionary is what we are left with at the close of the volume. Little wonder that this effort at a positive solution to a quarter decade of criticism was not exactly a highlight of Veblen's career.

One can draw a line from *The Vested Interests* to C. Wright Mills' *Power Elite*. It is a line that starts with the idea of the virtual monopoly of wealth and authority of the business class to a near conspiracy to bend and shape all aspects of society in its narrow image. It is a world in which notions of political democracy are virtually absent, and in which the people are served by marginalized groups like the International Workers of the World. Veblen knew full well that the common man was not simply the bearer of all virtue. But in identifying commonness with farmers who cultivate their own land, and factory workers who organize their own unions, Veblen was caught in the trap of populism. He wanted a virtuous outcome based on this common man, but on inspection was compelled to recognize that such common men were envious to the point of imitation of the businessman. Veblen, like Mills after him, saw no prospect of political struggle, party participation and voting patterns changing very much within the market system. Economic robbers must be fought with economic methods. As a result, the development of The New Deal and its allied varieties of liberalism were not anticipated by Veblen—for whom the Roaring Twenties was indeed the epitome and outcome of bourgeois decadence. Even if Veblen is now seen more as a sociologist than as an economist, he shared one characteristic of his professional tribe: a belief in the supremacy of a business civilization over a liberal state. Suffice it to say that these concerns remain very much part of our present-day policy agenda.

Irving Louis Horowitz

Preface

These papers have already appeared, in a slightly abridged form, in the *Dial*; running from the 19th October, 1918, to the 25th January, 1919, under the general caption: The Modern Point of View and the New Order. They are here reprinted in a collected form in response to requests which have come to hand. Except for a more detailed description at one point and another this text does not differ materially from the papers in the *Dial*. In point of scope and logical content this discussion resumes the argument of a course of lectures before students in Amherst College in May, 1918.

The aim of these papers is to show how and, as far as may be, why a discrepancy has arisen in the course of time between those accepted principles of law and custom that underlie business enterprise and the businesslike management of industry, on the one hand, and the material conditions which have now been engendered by that new order of industry that took its rise in the late 18th century, on the other hand; together with some speculations on the civil and political difficulties set afoot by this discrepancy between business and industry.

March, 1919

1

The Instability of Knowledge and Belief

As is true of any other point of view that may be characteristic of any other period of history, so also the modern point of view is a matter of habit. It is common to the modern civilized peoples only in so far as these peoples have come through substantially the same historic experience and have thereby acquired substantially the same habits of thought and have fallen into somewhat the same prevalent frame of mind. This modern point of view, therefore, is limited both in time and space. It is characteristic of the modern historical era and of such peoples as lie within the range of that peculiar civilization which marks off the modern world from what has gone before and from what still prevails outside of its range. In other words, it is a trait of modern Christendom, of Occidental civilization as it has run within the past few centuries. This general statement is not vitiated by the fact that there has been some slight diffusion of these modern and Western ideas outside of this range in recent times.

By historical accident it happens that the modern point of view has reached its maturest formulation and prevails with the least faltering among the French and English-speaking peoples; so that these peoples may be said to constitute the center of diffusion for that system of ideas which is called the modern point of view. Outward from this broad center the same range of ideas prevail throughout Christendom, but they prevail with less singleness of conviction among the peoples who are culturally more remote from this center, increasingly so with each farther remove. These others have carried over a larger remainder of the habits of thought of an earlier age, and have carried them over in a better state of preservation. It may also be that these others, or some of them, have acquired habits of thought of a new order which do not

1

altogether fit into that system of ideas that is commonly spoken of as the modern point of view. That such is the case need imply neither praise nor blame. It is only that, by common usage, these remainders of ancient habits of thought and these newer preconceptions that do not fit into the framework of West-European conventional thinking are not ordinarily rated as intrinsic to the modern point of view. They need not therefore be less to the purpose as a guide and criterion of human living; it is only that they are alien to those purposes which are considered to be of prime consequence in civilized life as it is guided and tested by the constituent principles of the modern point of view

What is spoken of as a point of view is always a composite affair; some sort of a rounded and balanced system of principles and standards, which are taken for granted, at least provisionally, and which serve as a base of reference and legitimization in all questions of deliberate opinion. So when any given usage or any line of conduct or belief is seen and approved from the modern point of view, it comes to the same as saying that these things are seen and accepted in the light of those principles that modern men habitually consider to be final and sufficient. They are principles of right, equity, propriety, duty, perhaps of knowledge, belief, and taste.

It is evident that these principles and standards of what is right, good, true, and beautiful, will vary from one age to another and from one people to another, in response to the varying conditions of life; inasmuch as these principles are always of the nature of habit; although the variation will of course range only within the limits of that human nature that finds expression in these same principles of right, good, truth, and beauty. So also, it will be found that something in the way of a common measure of truth and sufficiency runs through any such body of principles that are accepted as final and self-evident at any given time and place, in case this habitual body of principles has reached such a degree of poise and consistency that they can fairly be said to constitute a stable point of view. It is only because there is such a degree of consistency and such a common measure of validity among the commonly accepted principles of conduct and belief today, that it is possible to speak intelligently of the modern point of view, and to contrast it with any other point of view which may have prevailed earlier or elsewhere, as, e. g., in the Middle Ages or in Pagan Antiquity.

The Romans were given to saying, *Tempora mutantur,* and the Spanish have learned to speak indulgently in the name of *Costumbres del pals.* The common law of the English-speaking peoples does not coincide at all points with what was indefeasible right and good in the eyes of the Romans; and still less do its principles countenance all the vagaries of the Mosaic code. Yet, each and several, in their due time and institutional setting, these have all been tried and found valid and have approved themselves as securely and eternally right and good in principle.

Evidently these principles, which so are made to serve as standards of validity in law and custom, knowledge and belief, are of the nature of canons, established rules, and have the authority of precedent, prescription. They have been defined by the attrition of use and wont and disputation, and they are accepted in a somewhat deliberate manner by common consent, and are upheld by a deliberate public opinion as to what is right and seemly. In the popular apprehension, and indeed in the apprehension of the trained jurists and scholars for the time being, these constituent principles of the accepted point of view are "fundamentally and eternally right and good." But this perpetuity with which they so are habitually invested in the popular apprehension, in their time, is evidently such a qualified perpetuity only as belongs to any settled outgrowth of use and wont. They are of an institutional character and they are endowed with that degree of perpetuity only that belongs to any institution. So soon as a marked change of circumstances comes on, a change of a sufficiently profound, enduring and comprehensive character, such as persistently to cross or to go beyond those lines of use and wont out of which these settled principles have emerged, then these principles and their standards of validity and finality must presently undergo a revision, such as to bring on a new balance of principles, embodying the habits of thought enforced by a new situation, and expressing itself in a revised scheme of authoritative use and wont, law and custom. In the transition from the medieval to the modern point of view, e. g., there is to be seen such a pervasive change in men's habitual outlook, answering to the compulsion of a new range of circumstances which then came to condition the daily life of the peoples of Christendom.

In this mutation of the habitual outlook, between medieval and modern times, the contrast is perhaps most neatly shown in the altered standards of knowledge and belief, rather than in the settled domain of law and morals. Not that the mutation of habits which then overtook the Western world need have been less wide or less effectual in matters of conduct; but the change which has taken effect in science and philosophy, between the fourteenth century and the nineteenth, e. g., appears to have been of a more recognizable character, more easily defined in succinct and convincing terms. It has also quite generally attracted the attention of those men who have interested themselves in the course of historical events, and it has therefore become something of a commonplace in any standard historical survey of modern civilization to say that the scheme of knowledge and belief underwent a visible change between the Middle Ages and modern times.

It will also be found true that the canons of knowledge and belief, the principles governing what is fact and what is credible, are more intimately and intrinsically involved in the habitual behavior of the human spirit than any factors of human habit in other bearings. Such is necessarily the case, because the principles which guide and limit knowledge and belief are the ways and means by which men take stock of what is to be done and by which they take thought of how it is to be done. It is by the use of their habitual canons of knowledge and belief, that men construct those canons of conduct which serve as guide and standards in practical life. Men do not pass appraisal on matters that lie beyond the reach of their knowledge and belief, nor do they formulate rules to govern the game of life beyond that limit.

So, congenitally blind persons do not build color schemes; nor will a man without an "ear for music" become a master of musical composition. So also, "the medieval mind" took no thought and made no provision for those later-arisen exigencies of life and those later-known facts of material science which lay yet beyond the bounds of its medieval knowledge and belief; but this "medieval mind" at the same time spent much thought and took many excellent precautions about things which have now come to be accounted altogether fanciful, things which the mature insight, or perhaps the less fertile conceit, of a more experienced age has disowned as being palpably not in accord with fact.

That is to say, things, which once were convincingly substantial and demonstrable, according to the best knowledge and belief of the medieval mind, can now no longer be discerned as facts, according to those canons of knowledge and belief that are now doing duty among modern men as conclusive standards of reality. Not that all persons who are born within modern times are thereby rendered unable to know and to believe in such medieval facts, e. g., as horoscopes, or witchcraft, or gentle birth, or the efficacy of prayer, or the divine right of kings; but, taken by and large, and in so far as it falls under the control of the modern point of view, the deliberate consensus of knowledge and belief now runs to the effect that these and other imponderables like them no longer belong among ascertained or ascertainable facts; but that they are on the other hand wholly illusory conceits, traceable to a mistaken point of view prevalent in that earlier and cruder age.

The principles governing knowledge and belief at any given time are primary and pervasive, beyond any others, in that they underlie all human deliberation and comprise the necessary elements of all human logic. But it is also to be noted that these canons of knowledge and belief are more immediately exposed to revision and correction by experience than the principles of law and morals. So soon as the conditions of life shift and change in any appreciable degree, experience will enforce a revision of the habitual standards of actuality and credibility, because of the habitual and increasingly obvious failure of what has before habitually been regarded as an ascertained fact. Things which, under the ancient canons of knowledge, have habitually been regarded as known facts, as e.g., witchcraft or the action of bodies at a distance will under altered circumstances prove themselves by experience to have only a supposititious reality.

Any knowledge that runs in such out-worn terms turns out to be futile, misleading, meaningless; and the habit of imputing qualities and behavior of this kind to everyday facts will then fall into disuse, progressively as experience continues to bring home the futility of all that kind of imputation. And presently the habit of perceiving that class of qualities and behavior in the known facts is therefore gradually lost. So also, in due time the observances and the precautions and provisions embodied in law and custom for the preservation or the control of these lost imponderables will also fall into disuse and disappear out of the scheme of institutions, by way of becoming dead letter or by abrogation. Particularly will such a loss of belief and insight, and the consequent loss of those imponderables, whose ground has thereby gone out from under them, take effect with the passing of generations.

An Imponderable is an article of make-believe that has become axiomatic by force of settled habit. It can accordingly cease to be an Imponderable by a course of unsettling habit. Those elders in whom the ancient habits of faith and insight have been ingrained, and in whose knowledge and belief the imponderables in question have therefore had a vital reality, will presently fall away; and the new generation whose experience has run on other lines are in a fair way to lose these articles of faith and insight, by disuse. It is a case of obsolescence by habitual disuse. And the habitual disuse which so allows the ancient canons of knowledge and belief to fall away, and which thereby cuts the ground from under the traditional system of law and custom, is reinforced by the advancing discipline of a new order of experience, which exacts an habitual apprehension of workday facts in terms of a different kind and thereby brings on a revaluation and revision of the traditional rules governing human relations. The new terms of workday knowledge and belief, which do not conform to the ancient canons, go to enforce and stabilize new canons and standards, of a character alien to the traditional point of view. It is, in other words, a case of obsolescence by displacement as well as by habitual disuse.

This unsettling discipline that is brought to bear by workday experience is chiefly and most immediately the discipline exercised by the material conditions of life, the exigencies that beset men in their everyday dealings with the material means of life; inasmuch as these material facts are insistent and uncompromising. And the scope and method of knowledge and belief which is forced on men in their everyday material concerns will unavoidably, by habitual use, extend to other matters as well; so as also to affect the scope and method of knowledge and belief in all that concerns those imponderable facts which lie outside the immediate range of material experience. It results that, in the further course of changing habituation, those imponderable relations, conventions, claims and perquisites, that make up the time-worn system of law and custom will unavoidably also be brought under review and will be revised and reorganized in the light of the same new principles of validity that are found to be sufficient in dealing with material facts.

Given time and a sufficiently exacting run of experience, and it will follow necessarily that much the same standards of truth and finality will come to govern men's knowledge and valuation of facts throughout; whether the facts in question lie in the domain of material things or in the domain of those imponderable conventions and preconceptions that decide what is right and proper in human intercourse. It follows necessarily, because the same persons, bent by the same discipline and habituation, take stock of both and are required to get along with both during the same lifetime. More or less rigorously the same scope and method of knowledge and valuation will control the thinking of the same individuals throughout; at least to the extent that any given article of faith and usage which is palpably at cross purposes with this main intellectual bent will soon begin to seem immaterial and irrelevant and will tend to become obsolete by neglect.

Such has always been the fate that overtakes any notable articles of faith and usage that belong to a bygone point of view. Any established system of law and order will remain securely stable only on condition that it be kept in line or brought into line to conform with those canons of validity that have the vogue for the time being; and the vogue is a matter of habits of thought ingrained by everyday experience. And the moral is that any established system of law and custom is due to undergo a revision of its constituent principles so soon as a new order of economic life has had time materially to affect the community's habits of thought. But all the while the changeless native proclivities of the race will assert themselves in some measure in any eventual revision of the received institutional system; and always they will stand ready eventually to break the ordered scheme of things into a paralytic mass of confusion if it can not be bent into some passable degree of congruity with the paramount native needs of life.

What is likely to arrest the attention of any student of the modern era from the outset is the peculiar character of its industry and of its intellectual outlook, particularly the scope and method of modern science and technology. The intellectual life of democratic Europe and its cultural dependencies differs notably from what has gone before. There is all about it an air of matter-of-fact both in its technology and in its science; which culminates in a "mechanical conception" of all those things with which scientific inquiry is concerned about in the light of which many of the dread realities of the Middle Ages look like superfluous make-believe.

But it has been only during the later decades of the modern era—during that time interval that might fairly be called the post-modern era—that this mechanistic conception of things has begun seriously to affect the current system of knowledge and belief; and it has not hitherto seriously taken effect, except in technology and in the material sciences. So that it has not hitherto seriously invaded the established scheme of institutional arrangements, the stem of law and custom, which governs the relations of men to one another and defines their mutual rights, obligations, advantages and disabilities. But it should reasonably be expected that this established system of rights, duties, proprieties and disabilities will also in due time come in for something in the way of a revision, to bring it all more nearly into congruity with that matter-of-fact conception of things that lies at the root of the late-modern civilization.

The constituent principles of the established system of law and custom are of the nature of imponderables, of course; but they are imponderables which have been conceived and formulated in terms of a different order from those that are convincing to the twentieth-century scientists and engineers. Whereas the line of advance of the scientists and engineers, dominated by their mechanistic conception of things, appears to be the main line of march for modern civilization. It should seem reasonable to expect, therefore, that the scheme of law and custom will also fall into line with this mechanistic conception that appears to mark the apex of growth in modern intellectual life. But hitherto the "due time" needed for the adjustment has apparently not been had, or perhaps the experience which drives men in the direction of a mechanistic conception of all things has not hitherto been driving them hard enough or unremittingly enough to carry such a revision of ideas out in the system of law and custom. The modern point of view in matters of law and custom appears to be somewhat in arrears, as measured by the later advance in science and technology.

But just now the attention of thoughtful men centers on questions of practical concern, questions of law and usage, brought to a focus by the flagrant miscarriage of that organization of Christendom that has brought the War upon the civilized nations. The paramount question just now is, what to do to save the civilized nations from irretrievable disaster, and what further may be accomplished by taking thought so that no similar epoch of calamities shall be put in train for the next generation. It is realized that there must be something in the way of a "reconstruction" of the scheme of things; and it is also realized, though more dimly, that the reconstruction must be carried out with a view to the security of life under such conditions as men will put up with, rather than with a view to the impeccable preservation of the received scheme of law and custom. All of which is only saying that the constituent principles of the modern point of view are to be taken under advisement, reviewed and—conceivably—revised and brought into line, in so far as these principles are constituent elements of that received scheme of law and custom that is spoken of as the *status quo*. It is the *status quo* in respect of law and custom, not in respect of science and technology or of knowledge and belief, that is to be brought under review. Law and custom, it is believed, may be revised to meet the requirements of civilized men's knowledge and belief; but no man of sound mind hopes to revise the modern system of knowledge and belief so as to bring it all into conformity with the time-worn scheme of law and custom of the *status quo*.

Therefore the bearing of this stabilized modern point of view, stabilized in the eighteenth century, on these questions of practical concern is of present interest—its practical value as ground for a reasonably hopeful reconstruction of the war-shattered scheme of use and wont; its possible serviceability as a basis of enduring settlement; as well as the share which its constituent principles have had in the creation of that *status quo* out of which this epoch of calamities has been precipitated. The *status quo ante,* in which the roots of this growth of misfortunes and impossibilities are to be found, lies within the modern era, of course, and it is nowise to be decried as an alien, or even as an unforeseen, outgrowth of this modern era. By and large, this eighteenth-century stabilized modern point of view has governed men's dealings within this era, and its constituent principles of right and honest living must therefore, presumptively, be held answerable for the disastrous event of it all—at least to the extent that they have permissively countenanced the growth of those sinister conditions which have now ripened into a state of world-wide shame and confusion.

How and how far is this modern point of view, this body of legal and moral principles established in the eighteenth century, to be accounted an accessory to this crime? And if it be argued that this complication of atrocities has come on, not because of these principles of conduct which are so dear to civilized men and so blameless in their sight, but only in spite of them; then, what is the particular weakness or shortcoming inherent in this body of principles which has allowed such a growth of malignant conditions to go on and gather head? If the modern point of view, these settled principles of conduct by which modern men collectively are actuated in what they will do and in what they will permit, —if these canons and standards of clean and honest living have proved to be a fatal snare; then it becomes an urgent question: Is it safe, or sane to go into the future by the light of these same established canons of right, equity, and propriety that so have been tried and found wanting?

Perhaps the question should rather take the less didactic form: Will the present experience of calamities induce men to revise these established principles of conduct, and the specifications of the code based on them, so effectually as to guard against any chance of return to the same desperate situation in the calculable future? Can the discipline of recent experience and the insight bred by the new order of knowledge and belief, reinforced by the shock of the present miscarriage, be counted on to bring such a revision of these principles of law and custom as will preclude a return to that *status quo ante* from which this miscarriage of civilization has resulted? The latter question is more to the point. History teaches that men taken collectively, learn by habituation rather than by precept and reflection; particularly as touches those underlying principles of truth and validity on which the effectual scheme of law and custom finally rests.

In the last analysis it resolves itself into a question as to how and how far the habituation of the recent past, mobilized by the shock of the present conjuncture, will have affected the frame of mind of the common man in these civilized countries; for in the last analysis and with due allowance for a margin of tolerance it is the frame of mind of the common man that makes the foundation of society in the modern world; even though the elder statesmen continue to direct its motions from day to day by the light of those principles that were found good some time before yesterday. And the fortunes of the civilized world, for good or ill, have come to turn on the deeds of commission and of omission of these advanced peoples among whom the frame of mind of the common man is the finally conditioning circumstance in what may safely be done or left undone. The advice and consent of the common run has latterly come to be indispensable to the conduct of affairs among civilized men, somewhat in the same degree in which the community is to be accounted a civilized people. It is indispensable at least in a permissive way, at least to the extent that no line of policy can long be pursued successfully without the permissive tolerance of the common run; and the margin of tolerance in the case appears to be narrower the more alert and the more matter-of-fact the frame of mind of the common man.

2

The Stability of Law and Custom

In so far as concerns the present question, that is to say as regards those standards and principles which underlie the established system of law and custom, the modern point of view was stabilized and given as a definitive formulation in the eighteenth century; and in so far as concerns the subsequent conduct of practical affairs, its constituent principles have stood over without material change or revision since that time. So that for practical purposes it is fair to say that the modern point of view is now some one hundred and fifty years old.

It will not do to say that it is that much behind the times; because its timeworn standards of truth and validity are a very material factor in the makeup of "our time". That such is the case is due in great part to the fact that this body of principles was stabilized at that time and that they have therefore stood over intact, in spite of other changes that have taken place. It is only that the principles which had been tested and found good under the conditions of life in the modern era up to that time were at that time held fast, canvassed, defined, approved, and stabilized by being reduced to documentary form. In some sense they were then written into the constitution of civilized society, and they have continued to make up the nucleus of the document from that time forth; and so they have become inflexible, after the fashion of written constitutions.

In the sight of those generations who so achieved the definite acceptance of these enlightened modern principles, and who finally made good their formal installation in law and usage as self-balanced canons of human conduct, the principles which they so arrived at had all the sanction of Natural Law—impersonal, dispassionate, indefeasible and immutable; fundamentally and eternally right and good. That generation of men held "these truths to be self-evident"; and they have continued so to be held since that epoch by all those peoples who make up the effectual body of modern civilization. And the backward peoples, those others who have since then been coming into line and making their claim to a place in the scheme of modern civilized life, have also successively been accepting and (passably) assimilating the same enlightened principles of clean and honest living. Christendom, as a going concern of civilized peoples, has continued to regulate its affairs by the help of these principles, which are still held to be a competent formulation of the aspirations of civilized mankind. So that these modern principles of the eighteenth century, stabilized in documentary form a hundred and fifty years ago, have stood over in immutable perfection until our time—a monument more enduring than brass.

These principles are of the nature of habits of thought, of course; and it is the nature of habits of thought forever to shift and change in response to the changing impact of experience, since they are creatures of habituation. But inasmuch as they have once been stabilized in a thoroughly competent fashion in the eighteenth century, and have been drafted into finished documentary form, they have been enabled to stand over unimpaired into the present with all that weight and stability that a well-devised documentary formulation will give. It is true, so far as regards the conditions of civilized life during the interval that has passed since these modern principles of law and custom took on their settled shape in the eighteenth century, it has been a period of unexampled change—swift, varied, profound and extensive beyond example. And it follows of necessity that the principles of conduct which were approved and stabilized in the eighteenth century, under the driving exigencies of that age, have not altogether escaped the complications of changing circumstances. They have at least come in for some shrewd interpretation in the course of the nineteenth century. There have been refinements of definition, extensions of application, scrutiny and exposition of implications, as new exigencies have arisen and the established canons have been required to cover unforeseen contingencies; but it has all been done with the explicit reservation that no material innovation shall be allowed to touch the legacy of modern principles handed down from the eighteenth century, and that the vital system of Natural Rights installed in the eighteenth century must not be deranged at any point or at any cost.

It is scarcely necessary to describe this modern system of principles that still continues to govern human intercourse among the civilized peoples, or to attempt an exposition of its constituent articles. It is all to be had in exemplary form, ably incorporated in such familiar documents as the American Declaration of Independence, the French Declaration of the Rights of Man, and the American Constitution; and it is all to be found set forth with all the circumstance of philosophical and juristic scholarship in the best work of such writers as John Locke, Montesquieu, Adam Smith, or Blackstone. It has all been sufficiently canvassed, through all its dips, spurs and angles, by the most competent authorities, who have brought their best will and their best abilities to bear on its elucidation at every point, with full documentation. Besides which, there is no need of recondite exposition for the present purpose; since all that is required by the present argument is such a degree of information on these matters as is familiar to English-speaking persons by common notoriety.

At the same time it may be to the purpose to call to mind that this secular profession of faith enters creatively into that established order of things which has now fallen into a state of havoc because it does not meet the requirements of the new order. This eighteenth-century modern plan specifically makes provision for certain untoward rights, perquisites and disabilities which have, in the course of time and shifting circumstance, become incompatible with continued peace on earth and good-will among men.

There are two main counts included in this modern—eighteenth-century—plan, which appear unremittingly to make for discomfort and dissension under the conditions offered by the New Order of things:—National Ambition, and the Vested Rights of ownership. Neither of the two need be condemned as being intrinsically mischievous. Indeed, it may be true, as has often been argued, that both have served a good purpose in their due time and place; at least there is no need of arguing the contrary. Both belong in the settled order of civilized life; and both alike are countenanced by those principles of truth, equity and validity that go to make up the modern point of view. It is only that now, as things have been turning during the later one hundred years, both of these immemorially modern rights of man have come to yield a net return of hardship and ill-will for all those peoples who have bound up their fortunes with that kind of enterprise. The case might be stated to this effect, that the fault lies not in the nature of these untoward institutions of national sovereignty and vested rights, nor in those principles of self-help which underlie them, but only in those latterday facts which stubbornly refuse to fall into such lines as these forms of human enterprise require for their perfect and beneficent working. The facts, particularly the facts of industry and science, have outrun these provisions of law and custom; and so the scheme of things has got out of joint by that much, through no inherent weakness in the underlying principles of law and custom. The ancient and honorable principles of self-help are as sound as ever; it is only that the facts have quite unwarrantably not remained the same. The fault lies in the latter day facts, which have not continued in suitable shape. Such, in effect, has been the view habitually spoken for by many thoughtful persons of a conservative turn, who take an interest in concerting measures for holding fast that which once was good, in the face of distasteful facts.

The vested right of ownership in all kinds of property has the sanction of the time-honored principles of individual self-direction, equal opportunity, free contract, security of earnings and belongings, self-help, in the simple and honest meaning of the word. It would be quite bootless to find fault with these reasonable principles of tolerance and security. Their definitive acceptance and stabilization in the eighteenth century are among the illustrious achievements of Western civilization; and their roots lie deep in the native wisdom of mankind. They are obvious corollaries under the rule of Live and let live—an Occidental version of the Golden Rule. Yet in practical effect those vested rights which rest blamelessly on these reasonable canons of tolerance and good faith have today become the focus of vexation and misery in the life of the civilized peoples. Circumstances have changed to such effect that provisions which were once framed to uphold a system of neighborly good-will have now begun to run counter to one another and are working mischief to the common good.

Any impartial survey of the past one-hundred-fifty years will show that the constituent principles of this modern point of view governing the mutual rights and obligations of men within the civilized nations have held their ground, on the whole, without material net gain or net loss. It is the ground of Natural Rights, of self-help and free bargaining. Civil rights and the perquisites and obligations of ownership have remained substantially intact over this interval of a hundred and fifty years, but with some slight advance in the way of Live and let live at certain points, and some slight retrenchment at other points. So far as regards the formal stipulations, in law and custom, the balance or class interests within these countries has, on the whole, not been seriously disturbed. In this system of Natural Rights, as it has worked out in practice, the rights of ownership are paramount; largely because the other personal rights in the case have come to be a matter of course and so have ceased to hold men's attention.

So, in the matter of the franchise, e.g., the legal provisions more nearly meet the popular ideals of the modern point of view today than ever before. On the other hand the guiding principles in the case at certain other points have undergone a certain refinement of interpretation with a view to greater ease and security for trade and investment; and there has, in effect, been some slight abridgement of the freedom of combination and concerted action at any point where an unguarded exercise of such freedom would hamper trade or curtail the profits of business—for the modern era has turned out to be an era of business enterprise, dominated by the paramount claims of trade and investment. In point of formal requirements, these restrictions imposed on concerted action "in restraint of trade" fall in equal measure on the vested interests engaged in business and on the working population engaged in industry. So that the measures taken to safeguard the natural rights of ownership apply with equal force to those who own and those who do not. "The majestic equality of the law forbids the rich as well as the poor to sleep under bridges or to beg on the street corners." But it has turned out on trial that the vested interests of business are not seriously hampered by these restrictions; inasmuch as any formal restriction on any concerted action between the owners of such vested interests can always be got around by a formal coalition of ownership in the shape of a corporation. The extensive resort to corporate combination of ownership, which is so marked a feature of the nineteenth century, was not foreseen and was not taken into account in the eighteenth century, when the constituent principles of the modern point of view found their way into the common law. The system of Natural Rights is a system of personal rights, among which the rights of ownership are paramount; and among the rights of ownership is the right of free disposal and security of ownership and of credit obligations.

The same line of evasion is not available in the same degree for concerted action between persons who own nothing. Still, in neither case, neither as regards the owners of the country's wealth nor as regards the common man, can these restrictions on personal freedom of action be said to be a serious burden. And any slight mutilation or abridgement of the rule of self-help in their economic relations has been offset by an increasingly broad and liberal construction of the principles of self-direction and equality among men in their civil capacity and their personal relations. Indeed, the increasingly exacting temper of the common man in these countries during this period has made such an outcome unavoidable. By and large, in its formal vindication of personal liberty and equality before the law, the modern point of view has with singular consistency remained intact in the shape in which its principles were stabilized in the eighteenth century, in spite of changing circumstances. In point of formal compliance with their demands, the enlightened ideals of the eighteenth century are, no doubt, more commonly realized in practice today than at any earlier period. So that the modern civilized countries are now, in point of legal form and perhaps also in practical effect, more nearly a body of ungraded and masterless men than any earlier generation has known how to be.

In this modern era, as well as elsewhere and in other times, the circumstances that make for change; and reconstruction have been chiefly the material circumstances of everyday life—circumstances affecting the ordinary state of industry and ordinary intercourse. These material circumstances have changed notably during the modern era. There has been a progressive change in the state of the industrial arts, which has materially altered the scope and method of industry and the conditions under which men live in all the civilized countries. Accordingly, as a point of comparison, it will be to the purpose to call to mind what were the material circumstances, and more particularly the state of the industrial arts, which underlay and gave character to the modern point of view at the period when its constituent principles were found good and worked out as a stable and articulate system, in the shape in which they have continued to be held since then.

The material conditions of industry, trade and daily life during the period of transition and approach to this modern ground created that frame of mind which we call the modern point of view and dictated that reconstruction of institutional arrangements which has been worked out under its guidance. Therefore the economic situation which so underlay and conditioned this modern point of view at the period when it was given its stable form becomes the necessary point of departure for any argument bearing on the changes that have been going forward since then, or on any prospective reconstruction that may be due to follow from these changed conditions in the calculable future.

On this head, the students of history are in a singularly fortunate position. The whole case is set forth in the works of Adam Smith, with a comprehension and lucidity which no longer calls for praise. Beyond all other men Adam Smith is the approved and faithful spokesman of this modern point of view in all that concerns the economic situation which it assumes as its material ground; and his description of the state of civilized society, trade and industry, as he saw it in his time and as he wished it to stand over into the future, is to be taken without abatement as a competent exposition of those material conditions which were then conceived to underlie civilized society and to dictate the only sound reconstruction of civil and economic institutions according to the modern plan.

But like other men, Adam Smith was a creature of his own time, and what he has to say applies to the state of things as he saw them. What he describes and inquires into is that state of things which was to him the "historical present"; which always signifies the recent past—that is to say, the past as it had come under his observation and as it had shaped his outlook.

As it is conventionally dated, the Industrial Revolution took effect within Adam Smith's active lifetime, and some of its more significant beginnings passed immediately under his eyes; indeed, it is related that he took an active personal interest in at least one of the epoch-making mechanical inventions from which the era of the machine industry takes its date. Yet the Industrial Revolution does not lie within Adam Smith's "historical present," nor does his system of economic doctrines make provision for any of its peculiar issues. What he has to say on the-mechanics of industry is conceived in terms derived from an older order of things than that machine industry which was beginning to get under way in his own life-time; and all his illustrative instances and arguments on trade and industry are also such as would apply to the state of things that was passing, but they are not drawn with any view to that new order which was then coming on in the world of business enterprise.

The economic situation contemplated by Adam Smith as the natural (and ultimate) state of industry and trade in any enlightened society, conducted on sane and sound lines according to the natural order of human relations, was of a simple structure and may be drawn in few lines—neglecting such minor extensions and exceptions as would properly be taken account of in any exhaustive description. Industry is conceived to be of the nature of handicraft; not of the nature of mechanical engineering, such as it has in effect and progressively come to be since his time. It is described as a matter of workmanlike labor, "and of the skill, dexterity and judgment with which it is commonly applied." It is a question of the skilled workman and his use of tools. Mechanical inventions are "labor-saving devices," which "facilitate and abridge labor." The material equipment is the ways and means by manipulation of which the workman gets his work done. "Capital stock" is spoken of as savings parsimoniously accumulated out of the past industry of its owner, or out of the industry of those persons from whom he has legally acquired it by inheritance or in exchange for the products of his own labor. Business is of the nature of "petty trade" and the businessman is a "middle man" who is employed for a livelihood in the distribution of goods to the consumers. Trade is subsidiary to industry, and money is a vehicle designed to be used for the distribution of goods. Credit is an expedient of the needy; a dubious expedient. Profits (including interest) are justified as a reasonable remuneration for productive work done, and for the labor-saving use of property derived from the owner's past labor. The efforts of masters and workmen alike are conceived to be bent on turning out the largest and most serviceable output of goods; and prices are competitively determined by the labor cost of the goods.

Like other men Adam Smith did not see into the future beyond what was calculable on the data given by his own historical present; and in his time that later and greater era of investment and financial enterprise which has made industry subsidiary to business was only beginning to get under way and only obscurely so. So that he was still able to think of commercial enterprise as a middle-man's traffic in merchandise, subsidiary to a small-scale industry on the order of handicraft, and due to an assumed propensity in men "to truck, barter, and exchange one thing for another." And so much as he could not help seeing of the new order of business enterprise which was coming in was not rated by him as a sane outgrowth of that system of Natural Liberty for which he spoke and about which his best affections gathered. In all this he was at one with his thoughtful contemporaries.

That generation of public-spirited men went, perforce, on the scant data afforded by their own historical present, the economic situation as they saw it in the perspective and with the preconceptions of their own time; and to them it was accordingly plain that when all unreasonable restrictions are taken away, "the obvious and simple system of natural liberty establishes itself of its own accord." To this "natural" plan of free workmanship and free trade all restraint or retardation by collusion among businessmen was wholly obnoxious, and all collusive control of industry or of the market was accordingly execrated as unnatural and subversive. It is true, there were even then some appreciable beginnings of coercion and retardation—lowering of wages and limitation of output—by collusion between owners and employers who should by nature have been competitive producers of an unrestrained output of goods and services according to the principles of that modern point of view which animated Adam Smith and his generation; but coercion and unearned gain by a combination of ownership, of the now familiar corporate type, was virtually unknown in his time. So Adam Smith saw and denounced the dangers of unfair combination between "masters" for the exploitation of their workmen, but the modern use of credit and corporation finance for the collective control of the labor market and the goods market of course does not come within his horizon and does not engage his attention.

So also Adam Smith knows and denounces the use of protective tariffs for private gain. That means of pilfering was familiar enough in his time. But he spends little indignation on the equally nefarious use of the national establishment for safeguarding and augmenting the profits of traders, concessionaires, investors and creditors in foreign parts at the cost of the home community. That method of taxing the common man for the benefit of the vested interests has also grown to more formidable proportions since his time. The constituent principles of the modern point of view, as accepted advisedly or by oversight by Adam Smith and his generation, supply all the legitimation required for this larcenous use of the national establishment; but the means of communication were still too scant, and the larger use of credit was too nearly untried, as contrasted with what has at a later date gone to make the commercial ground and incentive of imperialist politics. Therefore the imperialist policies of public enterprise for private gain also do not come greatly within the range of Adam Smith's vision of the future, nor does the "obvious and simple system" on which he and his generation of thoughtful men take their stand comprise anything like explicit declarations for or against this later-matured chicane of the gentlemen-investors who have been managing the affairs of the civilized nations.

Adam Smith's work and life-time falls in with the high tide of eighteenth-century insight and understanding, and it marks an epoch of spiritual achievement and stabilization in civil institutions, as well as in those principles of conduct that have governed economic rights and relations since that date. But it marks also the beginning of a new order in the state of the industrial arts as well as in those material sciences which come directly in touch with the industrial arts and which take their logical bent from the same range of tangible experience. So it happens that this modern point of view reached a stable and symmetrical finality about the same date when the New Order of experience and insight was beginning to bend men's habits of thought into lines that run at cross purposes with this same stabilized point of view. It is in the ways and means of industry and in the material sciences that the new order of knowledge and belief first comes into evidence; because it is in this domain of workday facts that men's experience began about that time to take a decisive turn at variance with the received canons. A mechanistic conception of things began to displace those essentially romantic notions of untrammeled initiative and rationality that governed the intellectual life of the era of enlightenment which was then drawing to a close.

It is logically due to follow that the same general principles of knowledge and validity will presently undergo a revision of the same character where they have to do with those imponderable facts of human conduct and those conventions of law and custom that govern the duties and obligations of men in society. Here and now as elsewhere and in other times the stubborn teaching that comes of men's experience with the tangible facts of industry should confidently be counted on to make the outcome, so as to bring on a corresponding revision of what is right and good in that world of make-believe that always underlies any established system of law and custom. The material exigencies of the state of industry are unavoidable, and in great part unbending; and the economic conditions which follow immediately from these exigencies imposed by the ways and means of industry are only less uncompromising than the mechanical facts of industry itself. And the men who live under the rule of these economic exigencies are constrained to make their peace with them, to enter into such working arrangements with one another as these unbending conditions of the state of the industrial arts will tolerate, and to cast their system of imponderables on lines which can be understood by the same men who understand the industrial arts and the system of material science which underlies the industrial arts. So that, in due course, the accredited schedule of legal and moral rights, perquisites and obligations will also presently be brought into passable consistency with the ways and means whereby the community gets its living.

But it is also logically to be expected that any revision of the established rights, obligations, perquisites and vested interests will trail along behind the change which has taken effect in the material circumstances of the community and in the community's knowl-

edge and belief with regard to these material circumstances; since
any such revision of ancient rights and perquisites will necessarily
be consequent upon and conditioned by that change, and since the
axioms of law and custom that underlie any established schedule of
rights and perquisites are always of the nature of make-believe; and
the make-believe is necessarily built up out of conceptions derived from the accustomed range of knowledge and belief.

Out-worn axioms of this make-believe order become superstitions when the scope and method of workday knowledge has
outgrown that particular range of preconceptions out of which
these make believe axioms are constructed; which comes to saying that the underlying principles of the system of law and morals are therewith caught in a process of obsolescence—depreciation by supersession and disuse." By a figure of speech it might
be said that the community's intangible assets embodied in this
particular range of imponderables have shrunk by that much,
through the decay of these imponderables that are no longer sea-
sonable, and through their displacement by other figments of the
human brain—a consensus of brains trained into closer conso-
nance with the latterday material conditions of life. Something
of this kind, something in the way of depreciation by displacement, appears now to be overtaking that system of imponderables
that has been handed down into current law and custom out of
that range of ideas and ideals that had the vogue before the coming of the machine industry and the material sciences.

Since the underlying principles of the established order are of
this make-believe character, that is to say, since they are built up
out of the range of conceptions that have habitually been doing
duty as the substance of knowledge and belief in the past, it follows in the nature of the case that any reconstruction of institutions will be made only tardily, reluctantly, and sparingly; inasmuch as settled habits of thought are given up tardily, reluctantly
and sparingly. And this will particularly be true when the reconstruction of unseasonable institutions runs counter to a settled
and honorable code of ancient principles and a stubborn array of
vested interests, as in this instance. Such is the promise of the
present situation, and such is also the record of the shift that was
once before made from medieval to modern times. It should be a
case of break or bend.

3

The State of the Industrial Arts

The modern point of view, with its constituent principles of equal opportunity, self-help, and free bargaining, was given its definitive formulation in the eighteenth century, as a balanced system of Natural Rights; and it has stood over intact since that time, and has served as the unquestioned and immutable ground of public morals and expediency, on which the advocates of enlightened and liberal policies have always been content to rest in their case. The truths which it holds to be self-evident and indefeasible are conceived to be intrinsically bound up in an overruling Order of Nature; in which thoughtful men habitually believed at that time and in which less thoughtful men have continued to believe since then. This eighteenth-century order of nature, in the magic name of which Adam Smith was in the habit of speaking, was conceived on lines of personal initiative and activity. It is an order of things in which men were conceived to be effectually equal in all those respects that are of any decided consequence—in intelligence, working capacity, initiative, opportunity, and personal worth; in which the creative factor engaged in industry was the workman, with his personal skill, dexterity and judgment; in which, it was believed, the employer ("master") served his own ends and sought his own gain by consistently serving the needs of creative labor, and thereby serving the common good; in which the traders ("middle-men") made an honest living by supplying goods to consumers at a price determined by labor cost, and so serving the common good.

This characterization of the "obvious and simple system" that lies at the root of the liberal ideals may seem too much of a dream to any person who shuns "the scientific use of the imagination"; its imponderables may seem to lack that axiomatic self sufficiency which one would like to find in the spiritual foundations of a working system of law and custom. Indeed, the best of its imponderables are in a fair way now to drop back into the discard of uncertified make-believe. But in point of historical fact it appears to have stood the test of time and use, so far as appears formally on the face of law and custom. For a hundred years and more it has continued to stand as a familiar article of faith and aspiration among the advocates of a Liberal policy in civil and economic affairs; and Adam Smith's followers—the economists and publicists of the Liberal movement—have spoken for it as being the normal system of economic life, the "natural state of man," from which the course of events has been conceived to depart only under pressure of "disturbing causes," and to which the course of events must be pruned back at all hazards in the event of any threatened advance or departure beyond the "natural" bounds set by this working ideal.

However, the subsequent course of events has shown no indisposition to depart from this normal stem of economic life, this "natural state of man," on the effectual reality of which the modern point of view rests its inviolate principles of law and morals and economic expediency. A new order of things has been taking effect in the state of the industrial arts and in the material sciences that lie nearest to that tangible body of experience out of which the state of the industrial arts is framed. And the new order of industrial ways and means has been progressively going out of touch with the essential requirements of this established scheme of individual self-help and personal initiative, on the realization and maintenance of which the best endeavors of the Liberals have habitually been spent.

Under the new order the first requisite of ordinary productive industry is no longer the workman and his manual skill, but rather the mechanical equipment and the standardized processes in which the mechanical equipment is engaged. And this latter day industrial equipment and process embodies not the manual skill, dexterity and judgment of an individual workman, but rather the accumulated technological wisdom of the community. Under the new order of things the mechanical equipment—the "industrial plant"—takes the initiative, sets the pace, and turns the workman to account in the carrying-on of those standardized processes of production that embody this mechanistic state of the industrial arts; very much as the individual craftsman in his time held the initiative in industry, set the pace, and made use of his tools according to his own discretion in the exercise of his personal skill, dexterity and judgment, under that now obsolescent industrial order which underlies the eighteenth century modern point of view, and which still colors the aspirations of Liberal statesmen and economists, as well as the standard economic theories.

The workman—and indeed it is still the skilled workman—is always indispensable to the due working of this mechanistic industrial process, of course; very much as the craftsman's tools, in his time, were indispensable to the work which he had in hand. But the unit of industrial organization and procedure, what may be called the "going concern" in production, is now the outfit of industrial equipment, a works, engaged in a given standardized mechanical process designed to turn out a given output of standardized product; it is the plant, or the shop. And under this new order of industrial methods and values it has already come to be a commonplace of popular "knowledge and belief" that the mechanical equipment is the creative factor in industry, and the "production" of the output is credited to the plant's working capacity and set down to its account as a going concern; whereas the other factors engaged, as e. g., workmen and materials, are counted in as auxiliary factors which are indispensable but subsidiary—items of production-cost which are incorporated in the running expenses of the plant and its productive process.

Under the new order the going concern in production is the plant or shop, the works, not the individual workman. The plant embodies a standardized industrial process. The workman is made use of according as the needs of the given mechanical process may require. The time, place, rate, and material conditions of the work in hand are determined immediately by the mechanically standardized process in which the given plant is engaged; and beyond that all these matters are dependent on the exigencies and maneuvers of business, largely by way of moderating the rate of production and keeping the output reasonably short of maximum capacity. The workman has become subsidiary to the mechanical equipment, and productive industry has become subservient to business, in all those countries which have come in for the latter day state of the industrial arts, and which so have fallen under the domination of the price system.

Such is the state of things throughout in those greater industries that are characteristic of the New Order; and these greater industries now set the pace and make the standards of management and valuation for the rest. At the same time these greater industries of the machine era extend their domination beyond their own immediate work, and enforce a standardization of much the same mechanical character in the community at large; in the ways and means of living as well as in the ways and means of work. The effects of their mechanically standardized production, in the way of goods and services as well as in the similarly standardized traffic through which these goods and services are distributed to the consumers, reach out into the everyday life of all classes; but most immediately and imperatively they reach the working class of the industrial centers. So they largely set the pace for the ordinary occupations of the common man even apart from any employment in the greater mechanical industries. It is especially the latter-day system of transport and communication as it works out under the new order—highly mechanical and exactingly scheduled for time, rate and place—that so controls and standardizes the ordinary life of the common man on mechanical lines.

The training enforced by this mechanical standardization, therefore, is of much the same order throughout the community as it is within the mechanical industries proper, and it drives to the same outcome—submergence of the personal equation. So that the workday information and the reasoning by use of which all men carry on their daily life under the new order is of the same general character as that information and reasoning which guides the mechanical engineers; and the unremitting habituation to its scope and method, its principles of knowledge and belief, leads headlong to a mechanistic conception of things, ways, means, ends, and values, whether it is called by that name or not. The resulting frame of mind is often spoken of as Materialism. This impersonal character of workday habituation is particularly to be counted on to take decisive effect wherever the latter-day scheme of mechanical standardization takes effect with all that wide sweep and massive drift with which it now dominates the larger centers of population.

Since the modern era began, the state of the industrial arts has been undergoing a change of type, such as the followers of Mendel would call a "mutation." And in the course of this mutation the workman and his part in the conduct of industry have suffered as great a dislocation as any of the other factors involved. But it is also to be admitted that the typical owner-employer of the earlier modern time, such as he stood in the mind's eye of the eighteenth-century doctrinaires—this traditional owner-employer has also come through the period of the mutation in a scarcely better state of preservation. At the period of this stabilization of principles in the eighteenth century, he could still truthfully be spoken of as a "master," a foreman of the shop, and he was then still invested with a large reminiscence of the master-craftsman, as known in the time of the craft-gilds. He stood forth in the eighteenth-century argument on the Natural Order of things as the wise and workmanlike designer and guide of his workmen's handiwork, and he was then still presumed to be living in work-day contact and communion with them and to deal with them on an equitable footing of personal interest.

Such a characterization of the capitalist-employer who was doing business at the time of the Industrial Revolution may seem over-drawn; and there is no need of insisting on its precise accuracy as a description of eighteenth-century facts. But it should not be extremely difficult to show that substantially such a figure of an employer-owner was had in mind by those who then argued the questions of wages and employment and laid down the lines on which the employment of labor would be expected to arrange itself under the untroubled system of natural liberty. But what is more to the point is that which is beyond question. In practical fact, almost as fully as in the speculations of the doctrinaires, the employer of labor in the staple industries of that time was, in his own person, commonly also the owner of the establishment in which his hired workmen were employed; and also—again in passable accord with the facts—he was presumed personally to come to terms with his workmen about wages and conditions of work. Employment was considered to be a relation of man to man. That much is explicit in the writings which bear the date-mark of this modern Liberal point of view; and the same assumption has continued to stand over as a self-sufficient premise among the defenders of the free competitive system in industry, for three or four generations after that period.

But the course of events has gone its own way, and about that time—somewhere along in the middle half of the eighteenth century—that type of employer began to be displaced in those staple industries which have since then set the pace and made the outcome for wages and conditions of work. So soon as the machine industry began to make headway, the industrial plant increased in size, and the number of workmen employed in each establishment grew continually larger; until in the course of time the large scale of organization in industry has put any relation of man to man out of the question between employers and workmen in the leading industries. Indeed, it is not unusual to find that in an industrial plant of a large or middling size, a factory, mill, works, mine, shipyard or railway of the ordinary sort, very few of the workmen would be able, under oath, to identify their owner. At the same time, and owing to the same requirements of large-scale and mechanical organization, the ownership of the works has also progressively been changing character; so that today, in the large and leading industries, the place of the personal employer-owner is taken by a composite business concern which represents a combination of owners, no one of whom is individually responsible for the concern's transactions. So true is this, that even where the ownership of a given industrial establishment still vests wholly or mainly in a single person, it has commonly been found expedient to throw the ownership into the corporate form, with limited liability.

The personal employer-owner has virtually disappeared from the great industries. His place is now filled by a list of corporation securities and a staff of corporation officials and employees who exercise a limited discretion. The personal note is no longer to be had in the wage relation, except in those backward, obscure and subsidiary industries in which the mechanical reorganization of the new order has not taken effect. So, even that contractual arrangement which defines the workman's relation to the establishment in which he is employed, and to the anonymous corporate ownership by which he is employed, now takes the shape of a statistical reckoning, in which virtually no trace of the relation of man to man is to be found. Yet the principles of the modern point of view governing this contractual relation, in current law and custom, are drawn on the assumption that wages and conditions of work are arranged for by free bargaining between man and man on a footing of personal understanding and equal opportunity.

That the facts of the New Order have in this way departed from the ground on which the constituent principles of the modern point of view are based, and on which therefore the votaries of the established system take their stand, —this state of things can not be charged to anyone's personal account and made a subject of recrimination. In fact, it is not a case for personal discretion and responsibility in detail, but rather for concerted action looking to some practicable working arrangement.

The personal equation is no longer a material factor in the situation. Ownership, too, has been caught in the net of the New Order and has been depersonalized to a degree beyond what would have been conceivable a hundred years ago, especially so far as it has to do with the use of material resources and man power in the greater industries. Ownership has been "denatured" by the course of events; so that it no longer carries its earlier duties and responsibilities. It used to be true that personally responsible discretion in all details was the chief and abiding power conferred by ownership; but wherever it has to do with the machine industry and large-scale organization, ownership now has virtually lost this essential part of its ordinary functions. It has taken the shape of an absentee ownership of anonymous corporate capital, and in the ordinary management of this corporate capital the greater proportion of the owners have no voice.

This impersonal corporate capital, which is taking the place of the personal employer-owner of earlier times, is the outcome of a mutation of the scheme of things in business enterprise, scarcely less profound than the change which has overtaken the material equipment in the shift from handicraft methods to the machine technology. In practical fact today, corporate capital is the capitalized earning capacity of the corporation considered as a going business concern; and the ownership of this capital therefore foots up to a claim on the earnings of the corporation.

Corporate capital of this kind is impersonal in more than one sense: it may be transferred piecemeal from one owner to another without visibly affecting the management or the rating of the concern whose securities change hands in this way; and the personal identity of the owner of any given block of this capital need not be known even to the concern itself, to its administrative officers, or to those persons whose daily work and needs are bound up with the daily transactions of the concern. For most purposes and as regards the greater proportion of the investors who in this way own the corporation's capital, these owners are, in effect, anonymous creditors, whose sole effectual relation to the enterprise is that of a fixed "overhead charge" on its operations. Such is the case even in point of form as regards the investors in corporate bonds and preferred stock. The ordinary investor is, in effect, an anonymous pensioner on the enterprise; his relation to industry is in the nature of a liability, and his share in the conduct of this industry is much like the share which the Old Man of the Sea once had in the promenades of Sinbad.

No doubt, any reasonably skilful economist—any certified accountant of economic theory—could successfully question the goodness of this characterization of corporate capital. It is, in fact, not such a description as is commonly met with in those theories of ownership and investment that trace back to the formal definitions of Ricardo and Adam Smith. Nor is this description of latter-day facts here set down as a formal definition of corporate capital and its uses; nor is it designed to fit into that traditional scheme of conceptions that still holds the attention of the certified economists. Its aim is the less ambitious one of describing, in a loose and informal way, what is the nature and uses of this corporate capital and its ownership, in the apprehension of the common man out of doors. He is not so familiar with the recondite wisdom of the past, or with subtle definitions, other than the latter-day subtleties of the market, the crop season, the blast-furnace and refinery, the internal-combustion engine, and such like hard and fast matters with which he is required to get along from day to day. The purpose here is only to bring out, without undue precision, what these interesting phenomena of capital, investment, fixed charges, and the like, may be expected to foot up to in terms of tangible performance, in the unschooled reflections of the common man, who always comes in as "the party of the second part" in all these maneuvers of corporation finance. He commonly has no more than a slender and sliding grasp of those honorable principles of certified make-believe that distinguish the modern point of view in all that relates to property and its uses; but he has had the benefit of some exacting experience in the ways of the new order and its standards of reckoning. By consequence of much untempered experience the common man is beginning to see these things in the glaring though fitful light of that mechanistic conception that rates men and things on grounds of tangible performance—without much afterthought. As seen in this light, and without much afterthought, very much of the established system of obligations, earnings, perquisites and emoluments, appears to rest on a network of make-believe.

Now, it may be deplorable, perhaps inexcusable, that the New Order in industry should engender habits of thought of this unprofitable kind; but then, after all, regrets and excuses do not make the outcome, and with sufficient reason attention today centers on the outcome.

To the common man who has taken to reckoning in terms of tangible performance, terms of man power and material resources, these returns on investment that rest on productive enterprise as an overhead charge are beginning to look like unearned income. Indeed, the same unsympathetic preconception has lately come in for a degree of official recognition. High officials who are presumed to speak with authority, discretion and an unblessed mind have lately spoken of incomes from investments as "unearned incomes," and have even entertained a project for subjecting such incomes to a differential rate of taxation above what should fairly be imposed on "earned incomes." All this may, of course, be nothing more than an unseasonable lapse of circumspection on the part of the officials, who have otherwise, on the whole, consistently lived up to the best traditions of commercial sagacity; and a safe and sane legislature has also canvassed the matter and solemnly disallowed any such invidious distinction between earned and unearned incomes. Still, this passing recognition of unearned incomes is scarcely less significant for being unguarded; and the occurrence lends a certain timeliness to any inquiry into the source and nature of that net product of industry out of which any fixed overhead charges of this kind are drawn.

To come to an understanding of the source and origin of this margin of disposable revenue that goes to the earnings of corporate capital, it is necessary to come to an understanding of the industrial system out of which the disposable margin of revenue arises. Productive industry yields a margin of net product over cost, counting cost in terms of man power and material resources; and under the established rule of self-help and free bargaining as it works out in corporation finance, this margin of net product has come to rest upon productive industry as an overhead charge payable to anonymous outsiders who own the corporation securities.

There need be no question of the equity of this arrangement, as between the men at work in the industries and the beneficiaries to whom the overhead charge is payable. At least there is no intention here to question the equity of it, or to defend the arrangement against any question that may be brought. It is also to be remarked that the whole arrangement has this appearance of gratuitous handicap and hardship only when it is looked at from the crude ground level of tangible performance. When seen in the dry light of the old and honest principles of self-help and equal opportunity, as understood by the substantial and well-meaning citizens, it all casts no shadow of iniquity or inexpediency.

So, without prejudice to any ulterior question which may be harbored by one and another, the question which is here had in mind is quite simply as to the production of this disposable margin of net product over human cost. And to pass muster today, any attempted answer will be required to meet that exacting and often inconvenient insistence on palpable fact which is of the essence of the new order of knowledge and belief. It is necessary to reach an understanding of these things in terms of tangible performance, in such terms as are germane to that new order of knowledge and belief out of which the perplexity arises, rather than in those terms of equitable imputation that lie at the root of the certified economic doctrines and of corporation finance.

These relevant facts are neither particularly obscure nor particularly elusive; only, they have had little attention in the argument of economists and politicians. Still less in the speculations of the captains of finance. The partition of incomes has always been more easily understood by these practically-minded persons, and it is also a more engrossing subject of argumentation than the production of goods. This would be particularly true for these economists and politicians, who are imbued with that legalistic spirit which pervades the modern point of view and all its votaries.

But it is known to all, even to the most safely guarded persons who do not come in contact with industry or production, or even with the products of the staple industries, that industry at large will always turn out something in the way of a net margin of product over human cost—over human effort and necessary consumption. It holds true as far back as the records have anything to say. It is evidently a question of the productivity of the industrial arts. Men at work turn out a net product because they know how and are interested in doing it; and their output is limited by the industrial methods which they have the use of. But the output is limited in such a way that it always exceeds the cost by more or less, barring accident. By and large, throughout past time the industrial arts have been gaining in efficiency, and the ordinary margin of net product over cost has consequently gone on widening. This is much of the meaning of "an advance in the industrial arts."

In an earlier time, by law and custom, the net margin of product habitually went to a master class, so-called, as the "earnings" or the due emoluments of their mastery over those industrious classes who carried forward and gave effect to the state of the industrial arts as known in their time. By virtue of their mastery and its incorporation in the institutions of the time, they had an equitable, and effectual, vested interest in the net product of the community's industry; and by virtue of the same settled principles of law and custom it was for them to see to the due consumption of any such net product above cost. In later times, and particularly in modern times and in the civilized countries, those immemorial principles of privilege equitably vested in the master class have fallen into discredit as being not sufficiently grounded in fact; so that mastery and servitude are disallowed and have disappeared from the range of legitimate institutions. The enlightened principles of self-help and personal equality do not tolerate these things. However, they do tolerate free income from investments. Indeed, the most consistent and most reputable votaries of the modern point of view commonly subsist on such income.

Ever since these enlightened principles of the modern point of view were first installed in the eighteenth century as the self-evident rule of reason in civilized life, the industrial arts have also continued to gain in productive efficiency, at an ever accelerated rate of gain; so that today the industrial methods of the machine era are highly productive, beyond any earlier state of the industrial arts or anything that is known outside the range of this new order of industry. The output of this industrial system yields a wider margin of net product over cost than has ever been obtainable by any other or earlier known method of work. It consequently affords ground for an uncommonly substantial vested interest in this disposable net margin.

But the industrial system of the new order will work at the high rate of efficiency of which it is capable only under suitable conditions. It is a comprehensive system of interdependent working parts, organized on a large scale and with an exacting articulation of parts—works, mills, railways, shipping, groups and lines of industrial establishments, all working together on a somewhat delicately balanced plan of mutual give and take. No one member or section of this system is a self-sufficient industrial enterprise, even if it is true that no one member is strictly dependent on any other one. Indeed, no one member or section, group or line of industrial establishments, in this industrial universe of the new order, is a productive factor at all, except as it fits into and duly gives and takes its share in the work of the system as a whole. Such exceptions to this rule of interlocking processes as may appear on first examination, are likely to prove exceptions in appearance only. They are chiefly the backward trades and occupations which have not had the benefit of the Industrial Revolution and do not belong under the new, mechanistic order of industry; or they are trades, occupations and works devoted to the consumption of goods or to the maintenance of the rules governing the distribution and consumption of wealth, as, for instance, banking, menial service, police service and the apparatus of the law, the learned professions and the fine arts.

It is also of the essence of this industrial system and its technology that it necessarily involves the industrial community as a whole, its working population and its material resources; and the measure of its successful operation is determined by the effectual teamwork of its constituent parts. And the industrial system of the new order is drawn on a large scale and rests on a comprehensive specialization of processes and standardization of output; so that the "community" which is required for the necessary teamwork is necessarily a large community; larger than the total population and resources that would have served the like purpose under any earlier state of the industrial arts, at the same time that the needed coordination of processes is also wider and more delicately balanced than ever before. Indeed, the "industrial community" of the new order is always and necessarily larger than any existing national unit. The ramification of give and take under the new industrial system invariably overlaps the national frontiers, among all those peoples who occupy what would be called an "advanced" place in industry. The system, and therefore the industrial community engaged in teamwork under this system, is drawn on cosmopolitan or international lines, both in respect of the body of technological knowledge which is turned to account and in respect of the range and volume of materials necessary to be used according to this new order in productive industry.

Evidently the total output of product turned out under this industrial system, the "annual production," to use Adam Smith's phrase, or the "annual dividend," to use a phrase taken from later usage—this total output is the output of the total community working together as a balanced organization of industrial forces engaged in a moving equilibrium of production. No part or fraction of the community is a productive factor in its own right and taken by itself, since no work can be done by any segment of the community in isolation from the rest; no one plant or works would be a producer in the absence of all the rest. The total product is the product of the total community's work; or rather it is the product of the work of that fraction of the people who are employed in productive work—which is not quite the same thing, since there is much work spent on the consumption of goods, and on ways and means for such consumption, as well as on their production.

Indeed, it is by no means certain that there is not more time, strain and ingenuity spent on the consumption of goods than on their production. Apart from sports, menial service, fashionable dress and equipage, pet animals and mandatory social amenities, there would also have to be included under the ways and means of consumption virtually all that goes into salesmanship and advertising. Virtually all of these things have to do with the organized consumption of goods; and virtually all are therefore to be written off as waste motion, so far as regards their effect on the net productive efficiency of the industrial community, or of the industrial system whose tissues are consumed in enterprise of that kind. The amount which is to be written off as consumptive waste in this way is approximately the same as the net margin of product over cost; and according to the enlightened principles of self-help and equal opportunity, as these principles work out under the new order of industry, it is for the investors to take care of this consumptive waste and to see that no unconsumed residue is left over to cumber the market and produce a glut.

Evidently, too, the amount of the annual production depends on the state of the industrial arts which the working population has the use of for the time being; which is in the main a matter of technological knowledge and popular education. So that the question of productivity and net productivity may be stated in general terms to the following effect: The possible or potential productive capacity of any given community, having the disposal of a given complement of man power and material resources, is a matter of the state of the industrial arts, the technological knowledge, which the community has the use of; this sets the limit, determines the "maximum" production of which the community is capable. The actual production in such a community will then be determined by the extent to which the available technological efficiency is turned to account; which is regulated in part by the intelligence, or "education," of the working population, and in greater part by market conditions which decide how large a product it will be profitable for the businessmen to turn out. The net product is the amount by which this actual production exceeds its own cost, as counted in terms of subsistence, and including the cost of the necessary mechanical equipment; this net product will then approximately coincide with the annual keep, the cost of maintenance and replacement, of the investors or owners of capitalized property who are not engaged in productive industry; and who are on this account sometimes spoken of as the "kept classes." Indeed, it would seem that the number and average cost per capita of the kept classes, *communibus antis,* affords something of a rough measure of the net product habitually derived from the community's annual production.

The state of the industrial arts, therefore, is the indispensable conditioning circumstance which determines the productive capacity of any given community; and this is true in a peculiar degree under this new order of industry, in which the industrial arts have reached an unexampled development. The same decisive factor may also be described as "the community's joint stock of technological knowledge." This common stock of technological knowledge decides what will be the ordinary ways and means of industry, and so it decides what will be the character and volume of the output of product which a given man power is capable of turning out. Evidently no man power and no working population can turn out any annual product without the use of something in the way of technological knowledge, that is to say some state of the industrial arts. The working community is a productive factor only by virtue of, and only up to the limit set by, the state of the industrial arts which it has the use of. The contrast of industrial Japan or of industrial Germany before the middle of the nineteenth century and after the close of the century will serve for illustration; that is to say before and after those peoples had come in for the use of the technology of the machine era. The disposable excess of the yearly product over cost is a matter of the efficiency of the available state of technological knowledge, and of the measure in which the working population is put in a position to make use of it. These, of course, are obvious facts, which it should scarcely be necessary to recite, except that they are habitually overlooked, perhaps because they are obvious.

The Industrial Revolution of the eighteenth century was a revolution in the state of the industrial arts, of course; it was a mutation of character in the common stock of technological knowledge held and used by the industrial population of the civilized countries from that time forward. The shift from the older to the

new order of industry was of such a nature as to call for the use
of an extensive equipment of mechanical apparatus, progressively
more and more extensive as the change to the machine technology went on; and at the same time the disposable margin of product
above cost also progressively went on increasing with each further increase of the community's joint stock of technological
knowledge.

This body of technological knowledge, the state of the industrial arts, of course has always continued to be held as a joint
stock. Indeed this joint stock of technology is the substance of
the community's civilization on the industrial side, and therefore
it constitutes the substantial core of that civilization. Like any
other phase or element of the cultural heritage, it is a joint possession of the community, so far as concerns its custody, exercise, increase and transmission; but it has turned out, under the
peculiar circumstances that condition the use of this technology
among these civilized peoples, that its ownership or usufruct has
come to be effectually vested in a relatively small number of
persons. Unforeseen and undesigned, the mechanical circumstances of the new order in industry have reversed the practical
effects of the common law in respect of self-help, equal opportunity and free bargaining. The mechanics of the case has worked
out this result by cutting away the ground on which those principles were based at the time of their acceptance and installation.

The machine technology requires for its working a large and
specialized mechanical apparatus, an ever increasingly large and
increasingly elaborate material equipment. So also it requires a
large and diversified supply of material resources, both in raw
materials and in the way of motive power. It is only on condition
that these requirements are met in some passable fashion that
this industrial system will work at all, and it is only as these requirements are freely met that the machine industry will work at
a high efficiency. At the same time the settled principles of law
and usage and public policy handed down from the eighteenth
century have in effect decided, and continue to decide, that all
material wealth is, rightly, to be held in private ownership, and is
to be made use of only subject to the unhampered discretion of
the legally rightful owner. Meantime the highly productive state
of the industrial arts embodied in the technological knowledge

of the new order can be turned to account only by use of this material equipment and these natural resources which continue to be held in private ownership. From which it follows that these material means of industry, and the state of the industrial arts which these material means are to serve, can be turned to productive use only so far and on such conditions as the rightful owners of the material equipment and resources may choose to impose; which enables the owners of this indispensable material wealth, in effect, to take over the use of these industrial arts for their own sole profit. So that the usufruct of the community's technological knowledge has come to vest in the owners of such material wealth as is held in sufficiently large blocks for the purpose.

Therefore, by award of the settled principles of equity and self-help embodied in the modern point of view, as stabilized in the eighteenth century, the owners of the community's material resources—that is to say the investors in industrial business—have in effect become "seized and possessed of" the-community's joint stock of technological knowledge and efficiency. Not that this accumulated knowledge of industrial forces and processes has passed into the intellectual keeping of the investors and been assimilated into their mentality, even to the extent of a reasonably scanty modicum. It remains true, of course, that the investor, owners, kept classes, or whatever designation is preferred, are quite exceptionally ignorant of all that mechanics of industry whose usufruct is vested in them; they are, in effect, fully occupied with other things, and their knowledge of industry ordinarily does not, and need not, extend to any rudiments of technology or industrial process. It is not as intelligent persons, but only as owners of material ways and means, as vested interests, that they come into the case. The exceptions to this rule are only sufficiently numerous to call attention to themselves as exceptions.

As an intellectual achievement and as a working force the state of the industrial arts continues, of course, to be held jointly in and by the community at large; but equitable title to its usufruct has, in effect, passed to the owners of the indispensable material means of industry. Though not hitherto by formal specification and legal provision, their assets include, in effect, the state of the industrial arts as well as the mechanical appliances and the materials without which these industrial arts are of no effect. It is true, a little something, and indeed more than a little, has been done toward the due legal recognition of the investor's usufruct of the community's technological efficiency, in the recognition of vested interests and intangible assets as articles of private property defensible at law. But on the whole, and until a relatively recent date, the investors' tenure of this usufruct has been allowed to rest informally on their control of the community's material assets. Still, the outlook now appears to be that something further may presently be done toward a more secure and unambiguous tenure of this usufruct, by suitable legal decisions bearing on the inviolability of vested interests and intangible assets. The outcome is, in effect, that these owners have equitably become the sole legitimate beneficiaries of the community's disposable margin of product above cost.

These are also simple facts and patent, and they should seem sufficiently obvious without argument. They have also been explained at some length elsewhere. But this recital of what should already be commonplace information seems necessary here for the sake of a more perspicuous continuity in the present argument. To many persons, perhaps to the greater proportion of those unpropertied persons that are often spoken of collectively as "the common man," the state of things which has just been outlined may seem untoward. And further reflection on the character and prospective consequences of this arrangement is likely to add something more to the common man's apprehension of hardship and insecurity to come. Therefore it may be well to recall that this state of things has been brought to pass not by the failure of those principles of equity and self-help that lie at the root of it all, but rather by the eminently unyielding stability and sufficiency of these principles under new conditions. It is not due to any inherent weakness or shiftiness in these principles of law and custom; which have faithfully remained the same as ever, and which all men admit were good and sound at the period of their installation. But it is beginning to appear now, after the event, that the inclusion of unrestricted ownership among those rights and perquisites which were allowed to stand over when the transition was made to the modern point of view is likely to prove inexpedient in the further course of growth and change.

Unrestricted ownership of property, with inheritance, free contract, and self-help, is believed to have been highly expedient as well as eminently equitable under the circumstances which conditioned civilized life at the period when the civilized world made up its mind to that effect. And the discrepancy which has come in evidence in this later time is traceable to the fact that other things have not remained the same. The odious outcome has been made by disturbing causes, not by these enlightened principles of honest living. Security and unlimited discretion in the rights of ownership were once rightly made much of as a simple and obvious safeguard of self-direction and self-help for the common man; whereas, in the event, under a new order of circumstances, it all promises to be nothing better than a means of assured defeat and vexation for the common man.

4

Free Income

Industry of the modern sort—mechanical, specialized, standardized, drawn on a large scale—is highly productive. When this industrial system of the new order is not hindered by outside control it will yield a very large net return of output over cost—counting cost in terms of man power and necessary consumption; so large, indeed, that the cost of what is necessarily consumed in productive work, in the way of materials, mechanical appliances, and subsistence of the workmen, is inconsiderable by comparison. The same thing may be described by saying that the necessary consumption of subsistence and industrial plant amounts to but an inconsiderable deduction from the gross output of industry at any time. So inordinately productive is this familiar new order of industry that in ordinary times it is forever in danger of running into excesses and turning out an output in excess of what the market—that is to say the business situation—will tolerate. There is constant danger of "overproduction." So that there is commonly a large volume of man power unemployed and an appreciable proportion of the industrial plant lying idle or half idle. It is quite unusual, perhaps altogether out of the question, to let all or nearly all the available plant and man power run at full capacity even for a limited time.

It is, of course, impossible to say how large the net aggregate product over cost would be—counting the product in percentages of the necessary cost—in case this industrial system were allowed to work at full capacity and with free use of all the available technological knowledge. There is no safe ground for an estimate, for such a thing has never been tried, and no near approach to such a state of things is to be looked for under the existing circumstances of ownership and control. Even under the most favorable conditions of brisk times the business situation will not permit it. There will at least always be an indefinitely large allowance to be reckoned for work and substance expended on salesmanship, advertising, and competitive management designed to increase sales. This line of expenditures is a necessary part of businesslike management, although it contributes nothing to the output of goods, and in that sense it is to be counted as a necessary deduction from the net productive capacity of the industrial system as it runs. It would also be extremely difficult to make allowance for this deduction, since much of it is not recognized as such by the men in charge and does not appear on their books under any special descriptive heading. In one way and another, and for diverse and various reasons, the net production of goods serviceable for human use falls considerably short of the gross output, and the gross output is always short of the productive capacity of the available plant and man power.

Still, taken as it goes, with whatever handicap of these various kinds is to be allowed for, it remains patently true that the net product greatly exceeds the cost. So much so that whatever is required for the replacement of the material equipment consumed in production, plus "reasonable returns" on this equipment, commonly amounts to no more than a fraction of the total output. The resulting margin of excess product over cost plus reasonable returns on the material equipment is due to the high productive efficiency of the current state of the industrial arts and is the source of that free income which gives rise to intangible assets. The distinction between tangible assets and intangible is not a hard and fast one, of course, but the difference is sufficiently broad and sufficiently well understood for use in the present connection, so long as no pain is taken to confuse these terms with needless technical verbiage.

To avoid debate and digression, it may be remarked that "reasonable returns" is also here used in the ordinary sense of the expression, without further definition, as being sufficiently understood and precise enough for the argument. The play of motives and transactions by which a rough common measure of reasonable returns has been arrived at is taken for granted. A detailed examination of all that matter would involve an extended digression, and nothing would be gained for the argument.

According to the traditional view, which was handed on from the period before the coming of corporation finance, and which still stands over as an article of common belief in the certified economic theories, "capital" represents the material equipment, valued at its cost, together with funds in hand required as a "working capital" to provide materials and a labor force. On this view, corporation securities are taken to cover ownership of the plant and the needed working capital; and there has been a slow-dying prejudice against admitting that anything less tangible than these items should properly be included in the corporate capitalization and made a basis on which to issue corporate securities. Hence that stubborn popular prejudice against "watered stock" which corporation finance had to contend with all through the latter half of the nineteenth century. "Watered stock" is now virtually a forgotten issue. Corporation finance has disposed of the quarrel by discontinuing the relevant facts.

There is still a recognized distinction between tangible assets and intangible; but it has come to be recognized in corporation practice that the only reasonable basis of capitalization for any assets, tangible or intangible, is the earning-capacity which they represent. And the amount of capital is a question of capitalization of the available assets. So that, if the material equipment, e. g., is duly capitalized on its earning-capacity, any question as to its being "watered" is no longer worth pursuing; since stock can be said to be "watered" only by comparison with the cost of the assets which it covers, not in relation to its earning-capacity. The latter point is taken care of by the stock quotations of the market. On the other hand, intangible assets neither have now nor ever have had any other basis than capitalization of earning capacity, and any question of "water" in their case is consequently quite idle. Intangible assets will not hold water.

Corporation finance is one of the outgrowths of the New Order. And one of the effects wrought by corporation finance is a blurring of the distinction between tangible assets and intangible; inasmuch as both are now habitually determined by a capitalization of earning-capacity, rather than by their ascertained cost, and it is difficult, if not impossible, to draw a hard and fast line between that part of a concern's earning-capacity which is properly to be assigned to its plant and that which is due to its control of the market. Still, an intelligible distinction is maintained in common usage, between tangible assets and intangible, even if the distinction is somewhat uncertain in detail; and such a distinction is convenient, so long as too sharp a contrast between the two is not insisted on.

The earning-capacity of the tangible assets is presumed to represent the productive capacity of the plant, considered as a mechanical apparatus engaged in an industrial process for the production of goods or services; it is presumed to rest on the market value of the mechanical output of the plant. The plant is a productive factor because and in so far as it turns to practical account the state of the industrial arts now in use—the community's joint stock of technological knowledge. So soon, or so far, as the plant and its management falls short of meeting the ordinary requirements of this current state of the industrial arts, and fails to make use of such technological knowledge as is commonly employed, the whole works ceases by that much to be a productive factor. The productive efficiency, and the productive value, of any given item of industrial equipment is measured by its effective use of the technological knowledge current in the community for the time being. So also, the productive value of any given body of natural resources—land, raw materials, motive power—is strictly dependent on the degree in which it fits into the industrial system as it runs.

This dependence of productive value on conformity to and use of the state of the industrial arts is constantly shown in the case of land and similar natural resources, by the fluctuation of rental values. Land and other resources will be more valuable the more suitable they are for present and prospective use. The like is true for the mechanical equipment, perhaps in a more pronounced degree. Industrial plant, e. g., is always liable to depreciation by obsolescence in case the state of the industrial arts changes in such a way that the method of work embodied in the particular article of equipment is displaced by new and more suitable methods, more suitable under the altered circumstances. In such a case, which is of very frequent occurrence under the new order of industry, any given plant, machine, or similar contrivance may lose all its value as a means of production. And so also, on the other hand, a given plant, as, for instance, a given railway system or dock, may acquire additional productive value through changes in the industrial system which make it more suitable for present use.

Evidently the chief, or at least the indispensable, element of productive efficiency in any item of industrial equipment or resources is the use which it makes of the available technological knowledge; and evidently, too, its earning-capacity as a productive factor depends strictly on the same fact—the usufruct of the state of the industrial arts. And all the while the state of the industrial arts, which the industrial equipment so turns to account for the benefit of its owner, continues to be a joint stock of industrial knowledge and proficiency accumulated, held, exercised, increased and transmitted by the community at large; and all the while the owner of the equipment is some person who has contributed no more than his per-capita quota to this state of the industrial arts out of which his earnings arise. Indeed the chances are that the owner has contributed less than his per-capita quota, if anything, to that common fund of knowledge on the product of which he draws by virtue of his ownership, because he is likely to be fully occupied with other things—such things as lucrative business transactions, e. g., or the decent consumption of superfluities.

And at this point the difference between tangible assets and intangible comes in sight, or at least the ground of the habitual distinction between the two. Tangible assets, it appears, are such assets as represent the earning-capacity of any mechanically productive property; whereas intangible assets represent assured income which can not be assigned to any specific material factor as its productive source. Intangible assets are the capitalized value of income not otherwise accounted for. Such income arises out of business relations rather than out of industry; it is derived from advantages of salesmanship, rather than from productive work; it represents no contribution to the output of goods and services, but only an effectual claim to a share in the "annual dividend,"— on grounds which appear to be legally honest, but which can not be stated in terms of mechanical cause and effect, or of productive efficiency, or indeed in any terms that involve notions of physical dimensions or of mechanical action.

When the theoreticians explain and justify these returns that go to adroit salesmanship, or "managerial ability," as it is also called, it invariably turns but that the grounds assigned for it are of the nature of figures of speech—metaphor or analogy. Not that these standard theoretical explanations are to be set aside as faulty, inadequate or incomplete; their great volume and sincerity forbids that. It is rather that they are to be accepted as a faithful account of an insubstantial fact in insubstantial terms. And they are probably as good an account of the equitable distribution of free income as the principles of the modern point of view will tolerate.

But while intangible assets represent income which accrues out of certain immaterial relations between their owners and the industrial system, and while this income is accordingly not a return for mechanically productive work done, it still remains true, of course, that such income is drawn from the annual product of industry, and that its productive source is therefore the same as that of the returns on tangible assets. The material source of both is the same; and it is only that the basis on which the income is claimed is not the same for both. It is not a difference in respect of the ways and means by which they are created, but only in respect of the ways and means by which these two classes of income are intercepted and secured by the beneficiaries to whom they accrue. The returns on tangible assets are assumed to be a return for the productive use of the plant; returns on intangible assets are a return for the exercise of certain immaterial relations involved in the ownership and control of industry and trade.

Best known by name among intangible assets is the ancient rubric of "good-will," technically so called; which has stood over from before the coming of the new order in business enterprise. This has long been considered the original type-form of intangible assets as a class. By ancient usage the term denotes a customary preferential advantage in trade; it is not designed to describe a body of benevolent sentiments. Good-will has long been known, discussed and allowed for as a legitimate, ordinary and valuable immaterial possession of men engaged in mercantile enterprise of all kinds. It has been held to be a product of exemplary courtesy and fair dealing with customers, due to turning out goods or services of an invariably sound quality and honest measure, and indeed due to the conspicuous practice of the ordinary Christian virtues, but chiefly to common honesty. Similarly valuable, and of a similarly immaterial nature, is the possession of a trade-secret, a trade-mark, a patent right, a franchise, any statutory monopoly, or a monopoly secured by effectually cornering the supply or the market for any given line of goods or services. From any one of these a profitable advantage may be derived, and they have therefore a market value. They afford their possessor a preferential gain, as against his competitors or as against the general body of customers which the state of the industrial arts and the organization of business throws in his way. After the analogy of goodwill, it has been usual to trace any such special run of free income to the profitable use of a special advantage in the markeι, which is then appraised as a valuable means of gain and comes to figure as an asset of its possessor. But all this goes to explain how these benefits go to these beneficiaries; it does not account for the fact that there is produced a net output of product available for free distribution to these persons.

These supernumerary and preferential gains, "excess profits," or whatever words may best describe this class of free income, may be well deserved by these beneficiaries, or they may not. The income in question is, in any case, not created by the good deserts of the beneficiaries, however meritorious their conduct may be. Honesty may conceivably be the best policy in mercantile pursuits, and it may also greatly serve the convenience of any community in which an honest merchant is found; yet honest dealing, strictly speaking, is an agency of conservation rather than of creation. A trade secret may also be profitable to the concern which has the use of it, and the special process which it covers may be especially productive; but the same article of technological knowledge would doubtless contribute more to the total productivity of industry if it were shared freely by the industrial community at large. Such technological knowledge is an agency of production, but it is the monopoly of it that is profitable to its possessor as a special source of gain. The like applies to patent-rights, of course. Whereas monopolies of the usual kind, which control any given line of industry by charter, conspiracy, or combination of ownership, derive their special gains from their ability to restrain trade, limit the output of goods or services, and so "maintain prices."

Intangible assets of this familiar kind are very common among the business concerns of the new order, particularly among the larger and more prosperous of them, and they afford a rough measure of the ability of these concerns profitably to restrict production. The very large aggregate value of such assets indicates how imperative it is for the conduct of industrial business under the new order to restrict output within reasonable limits, and at the same time how profitable it is to be able to prevent the excessively high productive capacity of modern industry from outrunning the needs of profitable business. For the prosperity of business it is necessary to keep the output within reasonable limits; that is to say, within such limits as will serve to maintain reasonably profitable prices; that is to say such prices as will yield the largest obtainable net return to the concerns engaged in the business. In this connection, and under the existing conditions of investment and credit, "reasonable returns" means the same thing as "the largest practicable net returns." It all foots up to an application of the familiar principle of "charging what the traffic will bear"; for in the matter of profitable business there is no reasonable limit short of the maximum. In business, the best price is always good enough; but, so also, nothing short of the best price is good enough. Buy cheap and sell dear.

Intangibles of this kind, which represent a "conscientious withdrawal of efficiency," an effectual control of the rate or volume of output, are altogether the most common of immaterial assets, and they make up altogether the largest class of intangibles and the most considerable body of immaterial wealth owned. Land values are of much the same nature as these corporate assets which represent capitalized restriction of output, in that the land values, too, rest mostly on the owner's ability to withhold his property from productive use, and so to drive a profitable bargain. Rent is also a case of charging what the traffic will bear; and rental values should properly be classed with these intangible assets of the larger corporations, which are due to their effectual control of the rate and volume of production. And apart from the rental values of land, which are also in the nature of monopoly values, it is doubtful if the total material wealth in any of the civilized countries will nearly equal the total amount of this immaterial wealth that is owned by the country's businessmen and the investors for whom they do business. Which evidently comes to much the same as saying than something more than one-half of the net product of the country's industry goes to those persons in whom the existing state of law and custom vests a plenary power to hinder production.

It is doubtful if the total of this immaterial wealth exceeds the total material wealth in the advanced industrial countries; although it is at least highly probable that such is the case, particularly in the richer and more enlightened of these countries; as, e. g., in America or the United Kingdom, where the principles of self-help and free bargain have consistently had the benefit of a liberal—that is a broad—construction and an unbending application. The evidence in the case is not to be had in such unambiguous shape as to carry conviction, for the distinction between tangible assets and intangible is not consistently maintained or made a matter of record. So, e. g., it is not unusual to find that corporation bonds—railroad or industrial—which secure their owner a free income and are carried as an overhead charge by the corporation, are at the same time a lien on the corporation's real property; which in turn is likely to be of less value than the corporation's total liabilities. Evidently the case is sufficiently confusing, considered as a problem in the economic theory of capital, but it offers no particular difficulty when considered as a proposition in corporation finance.

There is another curious question that will also have to be left as a moot question, in the absence of more specific information than that which is yet available; more a question of idle curiosity, perhaps, than of substantial consequence. How nearly is it likely that the total gains which accrue to these prosperous business concerns and their investors from their conscientious withdrawal of efficiency will equal the total loss suffered by the community as a whole from the incidental reduction of the output? Net production is kept down in order to get a profitable price for the output; but it is not certain whether the net production has to be lowered by as much or more than the resulting increased gain which this businesslike strategy brings to the businesslike strategists. The strategic curtailment of net production below productive capacity is net loss to the community as a whole, including both the businessmen and their customers; the gains which go to these business concerns in this way are net loss to the community as a whole, exclusive of the business concerns and their investors. The resulting question is, therefore, not whether the rest of the community loses as much as the businessmen gain, — that goes without saying, since the gains of the businessmen in the case are paid over to them by the rest of the community in the enhanced (or maintained) price of the products; but rather it is a question whether the rest of the community, the common man, loses twice as much as the business concerns and their investors gain.

The whole case has some analogy with the phenomena of blackmail, ransom, and any similar enterprise that aims to get something for nothing; although it is carefully to be noted that its analogy with these illegitimate forms of gainful enterprise must, of course, not be taken to cast any shadow of suspicion on the legitimacy of all the businesslike sabotage that underlies this immaterial corporate capital and its earning-capacity. In the case of blackmail, ransom, and such like illegal traffic in extortion, it is known that the net loss suffered by the loser and the gainer together exceeds the net gain which accrues to the beneficiary, by as much as the cost of enforcement plus the incidental inconvenience to both parties to the transaction. At the same time, the beneficiary's subsequent employment and consumption of his "ill-gotten gains," as they are sometimes called, whether he consumes them in riotous living or in the further pursuit of the same profitable line of traffic, —all this, it is believed, does not in any degree benefit the rest of the community. As seen in the perspective of the common good, such enterprise in extortion is believed to be quite wastefully disserviceable.

Now, this analogy may be taken for what it is worth; "Analogies do not run on all-fours." But when seen in the same perspective, the question of loss and gain involved in the case of these intangible assets and their earning-capacity falls into something like this shape: Does the total net loss suffered by the community at large, exclusive of the owners of these intangibles, exceed two-hundred percent of the returns which go to these owners?' or, Do these intangibles cost the community more than twice what they are worth to the owners? —the loss to the community being represented by the sum of the overhead burden carried on account of these intangibles plus the necessary curtailment of production involved in maintaining profitable prices. The overhead burden is paid out of the net annual production, after the net annual production has been reduced by so much as may be necessary to "maintain prices at a reasonably profitable figure."

A few years ago any ordinarily observant person would doubtless have answered this question in the negative, probably without hesitation. So also, any ordinarily intelligent votary of the established order, as, e. g., a corporation lawyer, a commercial trade journal, or a trade-union official, would doubtless, at that period, have talked down such a question out of hand, as being fantastically preposterous. That would have been before the war experience began to throw light into the dark places of business enterprise as conducted under the new order of industry. Today (October, 1918)—it is to be admitted with such emotion as may come to hand—this question is one which can be entertained quite seriously, in the light of experience. In the recent past, as matters have stood up to the outbreak of the war, the ordinary rate of production in the essential industries under businesslike management has habitually and by deliberate contrivance fallen greatly short of productive capacity. This is an article of information which the experience of the war has shifted from the rubric of "Interesting if True" to that of "Common Notoriety."

The question as to how much this "incapacity by advisement" has commonly amounted to may be attempted somewhat after this fashion. Today, under compulsion of patriotic devotion, fear, shame and bitter need, and under the unprecedentedly shrew surveillance of public officers bent on maximum production, the great essential industries controlled by the vested interests may, one with another, be considered to approach—perhaps even conceivably to exceed—a fifty-percent efficiency; as counted on the basis of what should ordinarily be accomplished by use of an equally costly equipment having the disposal of an equally large and efficient labor force and equally good natural resources, in case the organization were designed and managed with an eye single to turning out a serviceable product, instead of, as usual, being managed with an eye single to private gain in terms of price.

To the spokesmen of "business as usual" this rating of current production under the pressure of war needs may seem extravagantly low; whereas, to the experts in industrial engineering, who are in the habit of arguing in terms of material cost and mechanical output, it will seem extravagantly high. Publicly, and concessively, this latter class will speak of 25 percent efficiency; in private and confidentially they appear disposed to say that the rating should be nearer to 10 percent than 25. To avoid any appearance of an ungenerous bias, then, present actual production in these essential industries may be placed at something approaching 50 percent of what should be their normal productive capacity in the absence of a businesslike control looking to "reasonable profits." It is necessary at this point to call to mind that the state of the industrial arts under the new order is highly productive, —beyond example.

This state of the case, that production in the essential industries presumably does not exceed 50 percent of the normal productive capacity, even when driven under the jealous eye of public officers vested with power to act, is presumably due in great part to the fact that these officers, too, are capable businessmen; that their past training and present bent is such as has been given them by long, exacting and successful experience in the businesslike management of industry; that their horizon and perspective in all that concerns industry are limited by the frame of mind that is native to the counting house. They, too, have learned how to think of industry and its administration in terms of profit on investment, and, indeed, in no other terms; that being as near as their daily work has allowed them to take stock of the ways and means of industry. So that they are still guided, in some considerable part, by considerations of what is decent, equitable and prudent in the sight of conservative businessmen; and this bias necessarily goes with them in their dealings with those ubiquitous, intricate and systematic dislocations of the industrial system which have been found profitable in the management of industry on a footing of competitive sabotage. They still find it reasonable to avoid any derangement of those vested interests that live on this margin of intangible assets that represents capitalized withdrawal of efficiency

In so characterizing the situation there is, of course, no inclination to impute blame to these businesslike officials who are patriotically giving their best abilities and endeavors to this work of enforcing an increased production in the essential industries and diverting needed labor and materials from the channels of waste; nor is it intended to cast aspersions on the good faith or the honorable motives of those grave captains of industry whom the officials find it so difficult to divert from the businessman's straight and narrow path of charging what the traffic will bear. "They are all honorable men." But like other men they are creatures of habit; and their habit of mind is the outcome of experience in that class of large, responsible and remunerative business affairs that lie somewhat remote from the domain of technology, from that field where the mechanistic logic of the industrial arts has something to say. It is only that the situation as here spoken of rests on settled usage, and that the usage is such as the businesslike frame of mind is suited to; at the same time that this businesslike usage, of fixed charges, vested interests and reasonable profits, does not fully comport with the free swing of the industrial arts as they run under the new order of technology. Nor is there much chance of getting away from this situation of "incapacity by advisement," even under pressure of patriotic devotion, fear, shame and need, inasmuch as the effectual public opinion has learned the same bias and will scarcely entrust the conduct of its serious interests to any other than businessmen and business methods.

To return to the argument. It may be conceded that production in the essential industries, under pressure of the war needs, rises to something like a 50 percent efficiency. At the same time it is presumably well within the mark to say that this current output in these essential industries will amount to something like twice their ordinary output in time of peace and business as usual. One-half of 50 percent is 25 percent; and so one comes in sight of the provisional conclusion that under ordinary conditions of businesslike management the habitual net production is fairly to be rated at something like one-fourth of the industrial community's productive capacity; presumably under that figure rather than over.

In the absence of all reflection this crude estimate may seem recklessly hasty, perhaps it may even be thought scandalously unflattering to our substantial citizens who have the keeping of the community's material welfare; but a degree of observation and reflection will quickly ease any feeling of annoyance on that score. So, e. g., if the account as presented above does not appear to foot up to as much as the conclusion would seem to require, further account may be taken of that side-line of business enterprise that spends work and materials in an effort to increase the work to be done, and to increase the cost per unit of the increased work; all for the benefit of the earnings of the concern for whose profit it is arranged. It may be called to mind that there still are half-a-dozen railway passenger stations in such a town as Chicago, especially designed to work at cross purposes and hinder the traffic of competing railway corporations; that on the basis of this ingeniously contrived retardation of traffic there has been erected a highly prosperous monopoly in the transfer of baggage and passengers, employing a large equipment and labor force and costing the traveling public some millions of useless outlay yearly; with nothing better to show for it than delay, confusion, wear and tear, casualties and wrangles, twenty-four hours a day; and that this arrangement is, quite profitably, duplicated throughout the country as often and on as large a scale as there are towns in which to install it. So again, there is an exemplary weekly periodical of the most widely reputable and most profitable class, with a circulation of more than two million, which habitually carries some 60 to 80 large pages of competitive advertising matter, at a time when the most exacting economy of work and materials is a matter of urgent and acknowledged public need; with nothing better to show for it than an increased cost of all the goods advertised, most of which are superfluities. This, too, is only a typical case, duplicated by the thousand, as nearly as the businesslike management of the other magazines and newspapers can achieve the same result. These are familiar instances of business as usual under the new order of industry. They are neither extreme nor extraordinary. Indeed the whole business community is run through with enterprise of this kind so thoroughly that this may fairly be said to be the warp of the fabric. In effect, of course, it is an enterprise in subreption; but in point of moral sentiment and conscious motive it is nothing of the kind.

All these intricate arrangements for doing those things that we ought not to have done and leaving undone those things that we ought to have done are by no means maliciously intended. They are only the ways and means of diverting a sufficient share of the annual product to the benefit of the legitimate beneficiaries, the kept classes. But this apparatus and procedure for capturing and dividing this share of the community's annual dividend is costly—one is tempted to say unduly costly. It foots up to, perhaps, something like one-half of the work done, and it is occupied with taking over something like one-half of the output produced by the remaining one-half of the year's work. And yet, as a business proposition it seems sound enough, inasmuch as the income which it brings to the beneficiaries will presumably foot up to something like one-half of the country's annual production.

There is nothing gained by finding fault with any of this businesslike enterprise that is bent on getting something for nothing, at any cost. After all, it is safe and sane business, sound and legitimate, and carried on blamelessly within the rules of the game. One may also dutifully believe that there is really no harm done, or at least that it might have been worse. It is reassuring to note that at least hitherto the burden of this overhead charge of 50 percent plus has not broken the back of the industrial community. It also serves to bring under a strong light the fact that the state of the industrial arts as it runs under the new order is highly productive, inordinately productive. And, finally, there should be some gain of serenity in realizing how singularly consistent has been the run of economic law through the ages, and recalling once more the reflection which John Stuart Mill arrived at some half-a-century ago, that, "Hitherto it is questionable if all the mechanical inventions yet made have lightened the day's toil of any human being."

5

The Vested Interests

There are certain saving clauses in common use among persons who speak for that well-known order of pecuniary rights and obligations which the modern point of view assumes as "the natural state of man." Among them are these: "Given the state of the industrial arts"; "Other things remaining the same"; "In the long run"; "In the absence of disturbing causes." It has been the praiseworthy endeavor of the votaries of this established law and custom to hold fast the good old plan on a strategic line of interpretation resting on these provisos. There have been painstaking elucidations of what is fundamental and intrinsic in the way of human institutions, of what essentially ought to be, and of what must eventually come to pass in the natural course of time and change as it is believed to run along under the guidance of those indefeasible principles that make up the modern point of view. And the disquieting incursions of the New Order have been disallowed as not being of the essence of Nature's contract with mankind, within the constituent principles of the modern point of view stabilized in the eighteenth century.

Now, as has already been remarked in an earlier passage, the state of the industrial arts has at no time continued unchanged during the modern era; consequently other things have never remained the same; and in the long run the outcome has always been shaped by the disturbing causes. All this reflects no discredit on the economists and publicists who so have sketched out the natural run of the present and future in the dry light of the eighteenth-century principles, since their reservations have not been observed. The arguments have been as good as the premises on which they proceed, and the premises have once been good enough to command unquestioning assent; although that is now some time ago. The fault appears to lie in the unexampled shifty behavior of the latter-day facts. Yet however shifty, these facts, too, are as stubborn as others of their kind.

The system of free competition, self-help, equal opportunity and free bargaining which is contemplated by the modern point of view, assumes an industrial situation in which the work and trading of any given individual or group can go on freely by itself, without materially helping or hindering the equally un-trammeled working of the rest. It has, of course, always been recognized that the country's industry makes up something of a connected system; so that there would necessarily be some de-gree of mutual adjustment and accommodation among the many self-sufficient working units which together make up the indus-trial community; but these working units have been conceived to be so nearly independent of one another that the slight measure of running adjustment needed could be sufficiently taken care of by free competition in the market. This assumption has, of course, never been altogether sound at any stage in the industrial ad-vance; but it has at least been within speaking distance of facts so late as the eighteenth century. It was a possible method of keeping the balance in the industrial system before the coming of the machine industry. Quite evidently it commended itself to the enlightened common sense of that time as a sufficiently work-able ideal. So much so that it then appeared to be the most prac-tical solution of the industrial and social difficulties which beset that generation. It is fairly to be presumed that the plan would still be workable in some fashion today if the conditions which then prevailed had continued unchanged through the interven-ing one hundred and fifty years, if other things had remained the same. All that was, in effect, before the coming of the machine technology and the later growth of population.

But as it runs today, according to the new industrial order set afoot by the machine technology, the carrying-on of the community's industry is not well taken care of by the loose cor-rective control which is exercised by a competitive market. That method is too slow, at the best, and too disjointed. The industrial system is now a wide-reaching organization of mechanical pro-cesses which work together on a comprehensive interlocking plan of give and take, in which no one section, group, or individual

unit is free to work out its own industrial salvation except in active co-partnership with the rest; and the whole of which runs on
as a moving equilibrium of forces in action. This system of interlocking processes and mutually dependent working units is a
more or less delicately balanced affair. Evidently the system has
to be taken as a whole, and evidently it will work at its full productive capacity only on condition that the coordination of its
interlocking processes be maintained at a faultless equilibrium,
and only when its constituent working units are allowed to run
full and smooth. But a moderate derangement will not put it out
of commission. It will work at a lower efficiency, and continue
running, in spite of a very considerable amount of dislocation;
as is habitually the case today.

At the same time any reasonably good working efficiency of
the industrial system is conditioned on a reasonably good coordination of these working forces; such as will allow each and
several of the working units to carry on at the fullest working
capacity that will comport with the unhampered working of the
system as a balanced whole. But evidently, too, any dislocation,
derangement or retardation of the work at any critical point—
which comes near saying at any point—in this balanced system
of work will cause a disproportionately large derangement of the
whole. The working units of the industrial system are no longer
independent of one another under the new order.

It is, perhaps, necessary to add that the industrial system has
not yet reached anything like the last degree of development along
this line; it is at least not yet a perfected automatic mechanism.
But it should also be added that with each successive advance
into the new order of industry created by the machine technol-
· ogy, and at a continually accelerated rate of advance, the processes of industry are being more thoroughly standardized, the
working units of the system as a whole demand a more undeviat-
ing maintenance of its moving equilibrium, a more exacting
mechanical correlation of industrial operations and equipment.
And it seems reasonable to expect that things are due to move
forward along this line still farther in the calculable future, rather
than the reverse.

This state of things would reasonably suggest that the control
of the industrial system had best be entrusted to men skilled in

these matters of technology. The industrial system does its work in terms of mechanical efficiency, not in terms of price. It should accordingly seem reasonable to expect that its control would be entrusted to men experienced in the ways and means of technology, men who are in the habit of thinking about these matters in such terms as are intelligible to the engineers. The material welfare of the community is bound up with the due working of this industrial system, which depends on the expert knowledge, insight, and disinterested judgment with which it is administered. It should accordingly have seemed expedient to entrust its administration to the industrial engineers, rather than to the captains of finance. The former have to do with productive efficiency, the latter with the haggling of the market.

However, by historical necessity the discretionary control in all that concerns this highly technological system of industry has come to vest in those persons who are highly skilled in the haggling of the market, the masters of financial intrigue. And so great is the stability of that system of law and custom by grace of which these persons claim this power, that any disallowance of their plenary control over the material fortunes of the community is scarcely within reason. All the while the progressive shifting of ground in the direction of a more thoroughly mechanistic organization of industry goes on and works out into a more and more searching standardization of works and methods and a more exacting correlation of industries, in an ever increasingly large and increasingly sensitive industrial system. All the while the whole of it grows less and less manageable by business methods; and with every successive move the control exercised by the businessmen in charge grows wider, more arbitrary, and more incompatible with the common good.

Business affairs, in the narrow sense of the expression, have in time necessarily come in for an increasing share of the attention of those who exercise the control. The businesslike manager's attention is continually more taken up with "the financial end" of the concern's interests; so that by enforced neglect he is necessarily leaving more of the details of shop management and supervision of the works to subordinates, largely to subordinates who are presumed to have some knowledge of technological matters and no immediate interest in the run of the market. They are in fact persons who are presumed to have this knowledge by the businessmen who have none of it. But the larger and final discretion, which affects the working of the industrial system as a whole, or the orderly management of any considerable group of industries within the general system, —all that is still under the immediate control of the businesslike managers, each of whom works for his own concern's gain without much afterthought. The final discretion still rests with the businesslike directorate of each concern—the owner or the board—even in all questions of physical organization and technical management; although this businesslike control of the details of production necessarily comes to little else than acceptance, rejection, or revision of measures proposed by the men immediately in charge of the works; together with a constant check on the rate and volume of output, with a view to the market.

In very great part the directorate's control of the industry has practically taken the shape of a veto on such measures of production as are not approved by the directorate for businesslike reasons, that is to say for purposes of private gain. Business is a pursuit of profits, and profits are to be had from profitable sales, and profitable sales can be made only if prices are maintained at a profitable level, and prices can be maintained only if the volume of marketable output is kept within reasonable limits; so that the paramount consideration in such business as has to do with the staple industries is a reasonable limitation of the output. "Reasonable" means "what the traffic will bear"; that is to say, "what will yield the largest net return."

Hence in the larger mechanical industries, which set the pace for the rest and which are organized on a standardized and more or less automatic plan, the current oversight of production by their businesslike directorate does not effectually extend much beyond the regulation of the output with a view to what the traffic will bear; and in this connection there is very little that the businessmen in charge can do except to keep the output short of productive capacity by so much as the state of the market seems to require; it does not lie within their competence to increase the output beyond that point, or to increase the productive capacity of their works, except by way of giving the technical men permission to go ahead and do it.

The businessman's place in the economy of nature is to "make money," not to produce goods. The production of goods is a mechanical process, incidental to the making of money; whereas the making of money is a pecuniary operation, carried on by bargain and sale, not by mechanical appliances and powers. The businessmen make use of the mechanical appliances and powers of the industrial system, but they make a pecuniary use of them. And in point of fact the less use a businessman can make of the mechanical appliances and powers under his charge, and the smaller a product he can contrive to turn out for a given return in terms of price, the better it suits his purpose. The highest achievement in business is the nearest approach to getting something for nothing. What any given business concern gains must come out of the total output of productive industry, of course; and to that extent any given business concern has an interest in the continued production of goods. But the less any given business concern can contrive to give for what it gets, the more profitable its own traffic will be. Business success means "getting the best of the bargain."

The common good, so far as it is a question of material welfare, is evidently best served by an unhampered working of the industrial system at its full capacity, without interruption or dislocation. But it is equally evident that the owner or manager of any given concern or section of this industrial system may be in a position to gain something for himself at the cost of the rest by obstructing, retarding or dislocating this working system at some critical point in such a way as will enable him to get the best of the bargain in his dealings with the rest. This appears constantly in the altogether usual, and altogether legitimate, practice of holding out for a better price. So also in the scarcely less usual, and no less legitimate, practice of withholding needed ground or right of way, or needed materials or information, from a business rival. Indeed it has been rumored that one of the usual incentives which drew the patriotic one-dollar-a-year men from their usual occupations to the service of their country was the chance of controlling information by means of which to "put it over" their business rivals. All these things are usual and a matter of course, because business management under the conditions created by the new order of industry is in great part made up of these things.

Sabotage of this kind is indispensable to any large success in industrial business.

But it is also evident that the private gain which the business concerns come in for by this management entails a loss suffered on the rest of the community, and that the loss suffered by the rest of the community is necessarily larger than the total gains which these maneuvers bring to the business concerns; inasmuch as the friction, obstruction and retardation of the moving equilibrium of production involved in this businesslike sabotage necessarily entails a disproportionate curtailment of output.

However, it is well to call to mind that the community will still be able to get along, perhaps even to get along very tolerably, in spite of a very appreciable volume of sabotage of this kind; even though it does reduce the net productive capacity to a fraction of what it would be in the absence of all this interference and retardation; for the current state of the industrial arts is highly productive. So much so that in spite of all this deliberate waste and confusion that is set afoot in this way for private gain, there still is left over an absolutely large residue of net production over cost. The community still has something to go on. The available margin of free income—that is to say, the margin of production over cost—is still wide; so that it allows a large latitude for playing fast and loose with the community's livelihood.

Now, these businesslike maneuvers of deviation and delay are by no means to be denounced as being iniquitous or unfair, although they may have an unfortunate effect on the conditions of life for the common man. That is his misfortune, which law and custom count on his bearing with becoming fortitude. These are the ordinary and approved means of carrying on business according to the liberal principles of free bargain and self-help as established in the eighteenth century; and they are in the main still looked on as a meritorious exercise of thrift and sagacity— duly so looked on, it is to be presumed. At least such is the prevailing view among the substantial citizens, who are in a position to speak from first-hand knowledge. It is only that the exercise of these homely virtues on the large scale on which business is now conducted, and when dealing with the wide-reaching articulations of the industrial system under the new order of technology—under these uncalled-for circumstances the unguarded exercise of these virtues entails business disturbances which are necessarily large, and which bring on mischievous consequences in industry which are disproportionately larger still.

It is also true, the businesslike managers of industrial enterprise have also other things to do, besides holding the marketable supply of goods and services down to such an amount as is expected to bring the most profitable prices, or diverting credulous customers from one seller to another by competitive advertising. But it should also be noted that there is next to no business enterprise, if any, whose chief end is not profitable sales, or profitable bargains which mean the same thing as profitable sales. They are therefore engaged unremittingly in one or another of the approved lines of competitive management with a view to profitable traffic for themselves, and to creating an advantage for themselves in the market. It is a poor-spirited concern that does not constantly aim to create for itself such a position of advantage as will give it something of a vested interest in the traffic. Such a concern is scarcely fit to survive; nor is it likely to.

It is not that business enterprise is wholly taken up with such like maneuvers of restraint, obstruction and competitive selling. This is only part of the businessmen's everyday work, although it is not a minor part. In any competitive business community this line of duties will take up a large share of the businessmen's attention and will engage their best and most businesslike abilities. More particularly in the management of the greater industrial enterprises of the present day, the larger as well as the more lucrative part of the duties of those who direct affairs appears commonly to be of this nature. That such should be the case lies in the nature of things under the circumstances which now prevail. It would not be far out of the way to say that any occupations in which this rule does not apply are occupations which have not, or have not yet, come into line as members in good standing in that new order of business enterprise which is based on the machine industry governed by the liberal principles of the eighteenth century.

"Our people, moreover, do not wait to be coached and led. They know their own business, are quick and resourceful at every readjustment, definite in purpose, and self-reliant in action....

The American businessman is of quick initiative. The ordinary and normal processes of private initiative will not, however, provide immediate employment for all of the men of our returning armies." Such is the esteem in which American businessmen are held by American popular opinion and such is also the view which American businessmen are inclined to take of their own place and value in the community. There need be no quarrel with it. But it will be in place to call attention to the statement that "The ordinary and normal processes of private initiative will not, however, provide immediate employment for all the men." It should be added, as is plain to all men, that these ordinary and normal processes of private initiative never do provide employment for all the men available. In fact, unemployment is an ordinary and normal phenomenon. So that even in the present emergency, when the peoples of Christendom are suffering privation together for want of goods needed for immediate use, the ordinary and normal processes of private initiative are not to be depended on to employ all the available manpower for productive industry. The reason is well known to all men; so well known as to be uniformly taken for granted as a circumstance which is beyond human remedy. It is the simple and obvious fact that the ordinary and normal processes of private initiative are the same thing as "business as usual," which controls industry with a view to private gain in terms of price; and the largest private gain in terms of price cannot be had by employing all the available manpower and speeding up the industries to their highest productivity, even when all the peoples of Christendom are suffering privation together for want of the ordinary necessaries of life. Private initiative means business enterprise, not industry.

But all the same, the profits of business come out of the product of industry; and industry is controlled, accelerated and slowed down with a view to business profits; and one outcome of this arrangement so far, in America, has been the complacent estimate of this business enterprise formulated in the passage quoted above. The result of a businesslike management of industry for private gain in America has on the whole been a fairly high level of prosperity. For this there are two main reasons: (a) the exceptionally great natural resources of their country; and (b) the continued growth and spread of population. (a) Business enterprise, that is to say private ownership, has taken over these resources, by a process of legalized seizure, and has used them up as rapidly as may be, with a view to private gain; all of which has gone to make private business profitable to that extent, although it has impoverished the underlying community by using up its natural resources. (b) The continued growth and spread of population, by natural increase and by immigration, has furnished the businessmen of this country a continually expanding market for goods; both for goods to be used in production and transportation and for finished articles of consumption. Hence the American businessmen have been in the fortunate position of not having to curtail the output of industry harshly and persistently at all points. It is, in effect, for this continued growth of their market, caused by the growth of population, that the businessmen claim credit when they "point with pride" to the resourcefulness and quick initiative with which they have "developed the country." To their credit be it said, they have on the whole not hindered the country's prosperity beyond what the traffic would bear; and the peculiar situation of this country hitherto has been such that the traffic of business would bear a nearly uninterrupted expansion of industry at perhaps something like one-half of its possible rate of expansion. To their own gain, and to the relief of the underlying community, they have been enabled profitably to let the country's industry run on a moderately high level of efficiency, — with more or less, but always a very appreciable amount, of unemployment, idle plant, and waste of resources.

All that industry which comes in under the dominant machine technology—that is to say all that fairly belongs in the new order of industry—is now governed by businessmen for business ends, in what is to be done and what is to be left undone. And wherever business enterprise has taken over the direction of things the management is directed in part to the production of a marketable supply, and in part to arranging for a profitable sale of the supply; and the strategy available for this latter, and indispensable, work lies almost wholly within the lines of competitive management already spoken of. In case these maneuvers of businesslike deviation and defeat are successful and fall into an orderly system whose operation may be continued at will, or in so far as this management creates an assured strategic advantage for any given business concern, the result is a vested interest. This may then eventually be capitalized in due form, as a body of intangible assets. As such it goes to augment the business community's accumulated wealth. And the country is statistically richer per capita.

A vested interest is a marketable right to get something for nothing. This does not mean that the vested interests cost nothing. They may even come high. Particularly may their cost seem high if the cost to the community is taken into account, as well as the expenditure incurred by their owners for their production and up-keep. Vested interests are immaterial wealth, intangible assets. As regards their nature and origin, they are the outgrowth of three main lines of businesslike management: (a) Limitation of supply, with a view to profitable sales; (b) Obstruction of traffic, with a view to profitable sales; and (c) Meretricious publicity, with a view to profitable sales. It will be remarked that these are matters of business, in the strict sense. They are devices of salesmanship, not of workmanship; they are ways and means of driving a bargain, not ways and means of producing goods or services. The residue which stands over as a product of these endeavors is in the nature of an intangible asset, an article of immaterial wealth; not an increase of the tangible equipment or the material resources in hand. The enterprising owners of the concern may be richer by that much, and so perhaps may the business community as a whole—though that is a precariously dubious point—but the community at large is no better off in any material respect.

This account, of course, assumes that all this business is conducted strictly within the lines of commercial honesty. It would only be tedious and misleading to follow up and take account of that scattering recourse to force or fraud that will never wholly be got rid of in the pursuit of gain, whether by way of business traffic or by more direct methods. Still, it may well be in place to recall that the code of commercial honesty applies only between the parties to a bargain, and takes no account of the interests of any third party, except by express injunction of the law; still less does it imply any degree of regard for the common good. Commercial honesty, of course, is the honesty of self-help, or *caveat emptor*, which is Latin for the same thing.

In the ordinary course of management some considerable amount of means and effort is spent in the pursuit of profitable sales and in creating or acquiring an advantage in their further pursuit. The enduring result, if any, is a body of intangible assets in the nature of what is called goodwill. The ordinary expenditure incurred for this purpose is so considerable in fact, that the "selling cost" will not infrequently be far and away the larger part of those costs that are to be covered by the price of advertised goods or advertised traffic. This necessary consumption of work and means with a view to increase sales and to create a prospective increase of profits is to be counted as net waste, of course; in the sense that it contributes nothing to the total output of serviceable goods, present or prospective. The net aggregate result is to lay equipment idle, hinder traffic, and induce credulous persons now and again to change their mind about what things they will buy.

Roughly, any business concern which so comes in for an habitual run of free income comes to have a vested right in this "income stream," and this preferred standing of the concern in this respect is recognized by calling such a concern a "vested interest," or a "special interest". Free income of this kind, not otherwise accounted for, may be capitalized if it promises to continue, and it can then be entered on the books as an item of immaterial wealth, a prospective source of gain. So long as it has not been embodied in a marketable legal instrument, any such item of intangible assets will be nothing more than a method of notation, a bookkeeper's expedient. But it can readily be covered with some form of corporation security, as, e.g., preferred stock or bonds, and it then becomes an asset in due standing and a vested interest endowed with legal tenure.

Ordinarily any reasonably uniform and permanent run of free income of this kind will be covered by an issue of corporate securities with a fixed rate of interest or dividends; whereupon the free income in question becomes a fixed overhead charge on the concern's business, to be carried as an item of ordinary and unavoidable outlay and included in the necessary cost of production of the concern's output of goods or services. But whether it is covered by an issue of vendible securities or carried in a less formal manner as a source of income not otherwise accounted for, such a vested right to get something for nothing will rightly be valued and defended against infraction from outside as a proprietary right, an item of immaterial but very substantial wealth.

There is nothing illegitimate or doubtful about this incorporation of unearned income into the ordinary costs of production on which "reasonable profits" are computed. "The law allows it and the court awards it." To indicate how utterly congruous it all is with the new order of business enterprise it may be called to mind that not only do the captains of corporation finance habitually handle the matter in that way, but the same view is accepted by those public authorities who are called in to review and regulate the traffic of the business concerns governed by these captains of finance. The later findings are apparently unequivocal, to the effect that when once a run of free income has been capitalized and docketed as an asset it becomes a legitimate overhead charge, and it is then justly to be counted among necessary costs and covered by the price which consumers should reasonably pay for the concern's offering of goods or services.

Such a finding has come to be a fairly well settled matter of course both among the officials and among the law-abiding investors, so far as regards those intangible assets that are covered by vendible securities carrying a fixed rate; and the logic of this finding is doubtless sound according to the principles of the modern point of view, which were put into stable form before the coming of corporation finance. There may still be a doubt or a question whether valuable perquisites of the same nature, which continue to be held loosely as an informal vested interest, as, e.g., merchantable goodwill, are similarly entitled to the benefit of the common law which secures any owner in the usufruct of his property. To such effect have commonly been the findings of courts and boards of inquiry, of Public Utility Commissions, of such bodies as the Interstate Commerce Commission, the Federal Trade Commission, and latterly of diverse recently installed agencies for the control of prices and output in behalf of the public interest; so, for instance, right lately, certain decisions and recommendations of the War Labor Board.

Any person with a taste for curiosities of human behavior might well pursue this question of capitalized free income into its further convolutions, and might find reasonable entertainment in so doing. The topic also has merits as a subject for economic theory. But for the present argument it may suffice to note that this free income and the businesslike contrivances by which it is made secure and legitimate are of the essence of this new order of business enterprise; that the abiding incentive to such enterprise lies in this unearned income; and that the intangible assets which are framed to cover this line of "earnings," therefore, constitute the substantial core of corporate capital under the new order. In passing, it may also be noted that there is room for a division of sentiment as regards this disposal of the community's net production, and that peremptory questions of class interest and public policy touching these matters may presently be due to come to a hearing.

To some, this manner of presenting the case may seem unfamiliar, and it may therefore be to the purpose to restate the upshot of this account in the briefest fashion: Capital—at least under the new order of business enterprise—is capitalized prospective gain. From this arises one of the singularities of the current situation in business and its control of industry; viz., that the total face value, or even the total market value of the vendible securities which cover any given block of industrial equipment and material resources, and which give title to its ownership, always and greatly exceeds the total market value of the equipment and resources to which the securities give title of ownership, and to which alone in the last resort they do give title. The margin by which the capitalized value of the going concern exceeds the value of its material properties is commonly quite wide. Only in the case of small and feeble corporations, or such concerns as are balancing along the edge of bankruptcy, does this margin of intangible values narrow down and tend to disappear. Any industrial business concern which does not enjoy such a margin of capitalized free earning capacity has fallen short of ordinary business success and is possessed of no vested interest.

This margin of free income which is capitalized in the value of the going concern comes out of the net product of industry over cost. It is secured by successful bargaining and an advantageous position in the market; which involves some derangement and retardation of the industrial system—so much so as greatly to reduce the net margin of production over cost. Approximately the whole of this remaining margin of free income goes to the businessmen in charge, or to the business concerns for whom this management is carried on. In case the free income which is gained in this way promises to continue, it presently becomes a vested right. It may then be formally capitalized as an immaterial asset having a recognized earning capacity equal to this prospective free income. That is to say, the outcome is a capitalized claim to get something for nothing; which constitutes a vested interest. The total gains which hereby accrue to the owners of these vested rights amount to something less than the total loss suffered by the community at large through that delay of production and derangement of industry that is involved in the due exercise of these rights. In other words, and as seen from the other side, this free income which the community allows its kept classes in the way of returns on these vested rights and intangible assets is the price which the community is paying to the owners of this imponderable wealth for material damage greatly exceeding that amount. But it should be kept in mind and should be duly credited to the good intentions of these businesslike managers, that the ulterior object sought by all this management is not the 100 per cent of mischief to the community but only the 10 per cent of private gain for themselves and their clients.

So far as they bear immediately on the argument at this point the main facts are substantially as set forth. But to avoid any appearance of undue novelty, as well as to avoid the appearance of neglecting relevant facts, something more is to be said in the same connection. It is particularly to be noted that credit for certain material benefits should be given to this same business enterprise whose chief aim and effect is the creation of these vested rights to unearned income. It will be apparent to anyone who is at all familiar with the situation, that much of the intangible assets included in the corporate capital of this country, e.g., does not represent derangement which is actually inflicted on the industrial system from day to day, but rather the price of delivery from derangement which the businesslike managers of industry have taken measures to discontinue and disallow.

A concrete illustration will show what is intended. For some time past, and very noticeably during the past quarter-century, the ownership of the large industrial concerns has constantly been drawing together into larger and larger aggregations, with a more centralized control. The case of the steel industry is typical. For a considerable period, beginning in the early nineties, there went on a process of combination and recombination of corporations in this industry, resulting in larger and larger aggregations of corporate ownership. Commonly, though perhaps not invariably, some of the unprofitable duplication and work at cross purposes that was necessarily involved in the earlier parcelment of ownership was got rid of in this way, gradually with each successive move in this concentration of ownership and control. Perhaps also invariably there was a substantial saving made in the aggregate volume of business dealings that would necessarily be involved in carrying on the industry. Under the management of many concerns each intent on its own pecuniary interest, the details of business transactions would be voluminous and intricate, in the way of contracts, orders, running accounts, working arrangements, as well as the necessary financial operations, properly so called. Much of this would be obviated by taking over the ownership of these concerns into the hands of a centralized control; and there would be a consequent lessening of that delay and uncertainty that always is to be counted on wherever the industrial operations have to wait on the completion of various business arrangements, as they habitually do. There is circumstantial evidence that very material gains in economy and expedition commonly resulted from these successive moves of consolidation in the steel business. And this discontinuance of businesslike delay and calculated maladjustment was at each successive move brought to a secure footing and capitalized in an increased issue of negotiable corporation securities.

It will also be recalled that, as a matter of routine, each successive consolidation of ownership involved a recapitalization of the concerns so brought together under a common head, and that commonly if not invariably the resulting recapitalization would be larger than the aggregate earlier capital of the underlying corporations. Even where, as sometimes has happened, there was no increase made in the nominal capitalization, there would still result an effectual increase; in that the market value of the securities outstanding would be larger after the operation than the value of the aggregate capital of the underlying corporations had been before. There has commonly been some gain in aggregate capitalization, and the resulting increased capitalization has also commonly proved to be valid. The market value of the larger and more stable capitalization has presently proved to be larger and more stable than the capitalization of the same properties under the earlier regime of divided ownership and control. What has so been added to the aggregate capitalization has in the main been the relative absence of work at cross purposes, which has resulted from the consolidation of ownership; and it is to be accounted a typical instance of intangible assets. The new and larger capitalization has commonly made good; and this is particularly true for those later, larger and more conclusive recombinations of corporate ownership with which the so-called era of trust-making in the steel business came to a provisional conclusion. The U.S. Steel Corporation has vindicated the wisdom of an unreserved advance on lines of consolidation and recapitalization in the financing of the large and technical industries.

For reasons well understood by those who are acquainted with these things, no one can offer a confident estimate, or even a particularly intelligent opinion, as to the aggregate amount of overhead burden and intangible assets which has been written into the corporate capital of the steel business in the course of a few years of consolidation. For reasons of depreciation, disuse, replacement, extension, renewal, changes in market conditions and in technical requirements, the case is too intricate to admit anything like a clear-cut identification of the immaterial items included in the capitalization. But there is no chance to doubt that in the aggregate these immaterial items foot up to a very formidable proportion of the total capital.

And what is true for the steel business in this respect will doubtless apply even more unreservedly in transportation, or in such a case as the oil business. The latter may be taken as a typical case, differing from steel in some of the circumstances which condition its business organization, but comparable with steel in respect of the necessity for a centralized control. In the oil business a rough classification of assets would take some such shape as this: (a) Monopolization of natural resources, (b) Control of markets by limitation of the supply, (c) Plant. Of these three, the last named, the material equipment, would unquestionably be found to be altogether the slightest and least valuable. What is not doubtful, in the steel business or in any of the other industrial enterprises that run on a similar scale and a similar level of technology, is that the owners of the corporate capital have come in for a very substantial body of intangible assets of this kind, and that these assets of capitalized free income will foot up to several times the total value of the material assets which underlie them.

It is evident that the businesslike management of industry under these conditions need not involve derangement and cross-purposes at every turn. It should always be likely that the businessmen in charge will find it to their profit to combine forces, eliminate wasteful traffic, allow a reasonably free and economical working of the country's productive powers within the limits of a profitable price, and so come in for a larger total of free income to be divided amicably among themselves on a concerted plan. This can be done by means of a combination of ownership, such as the corporations of the present time. But there is a difficulty of principle involved in this use of incorporation as a method of combining forces. Such a consolidation of ownership and control on a large scale appears to be, in effect, a combination of forces against the rest of the community or in contravention of the principles of free competition. In effect it foots up to the same thing as a combination in restraint of trade; in form it is a concentration of ownership. Combination of owners in restraint of trade is obnoxious to the liberal principles of free bargaining and self-help; consolidation of ownership by purchase or incorporation appears to be a reasonable exercise of the right of free bargaining and self-help. There is accordingly some chance of a difference of opinion at this point and some risk of playing fast and loose with these liberal principles that disallow conspiracy in restraint of trade. This difficulty of principle has been sought to be got over by believing that a combination of ownership in restraint of trade does not amount to a conspiracy in restraint of trade, within the purport of these liberal principles. There is a great and pressing need of such a construction of these principles, which would greatly facilitate the work of corporation finance; but it is to be admitted that some slight cloud still rests on this manner of disposing of ownership. It involves abdication or delegation of that discretionary exercise of property rights which has been held to be of the essence of ownership.

The new state of things brought about by such a consolidation is capitalized as a permanent source of free income. And if it proves to be a sound business proposition the new capitalization will measure the increase of income which goes to its promoter or to the corporation in whose name the move has been made; and if the work is well and neatly done, no one else will get any gain from it or be in any way benefited by the arrangement. It is a business proposition, not a fanciful project of public utility. The capitalized value of such a coalition of ownership is not measured by any heightened production or any retrenchment of waste that may come in its train, nor need the new move bring any saving or any addition to the community's net productive resources in any respect. Indeed, it happens not infrequently that such a waste-conserving coalition of ownership leads directly to a restriction of output, according to the familiar run of monopoly rule. So frequently will restriction, enhanced prices, unemployment, and hardship follow in such a case, that it has come to be an article of popular knowledge and belief that this is the logical aim and outcome of any successful maneuver of the kind.

So also, though its output of marketable goods or services may be got on easier terms, the new and larger business concern which results from the coalition need be no more open-handed or humane in its dealings with its workmen. There will, in fact, be some provocation to the contrary. A more powerful corporation is in a position to make its own terms with greater freedom, which it then is for the workmen to take or leave, but ordinarily to take; for the universal rule of businesslike management—to charge what the traffic will bear—continues to hold unbroken for any business concern, irrespective of its size or its facilities. As has already been noted in an earlier passage, charging what the traffic will bear is the same as charging what will yield the largest net profit.

There stand over two main questions touching the nature and uses of these vested interests: —Why do not these powerful business concerns exercise their autocratic powers to drive the industrial system at its full productive capacity, seeing that they are in a position to claim any increase of net production over cost? and, What use is made of the free income which goes to them as the perquisite of their vested interest? The answer to the former question is to be found in the fact that the great business concerns as well as the smaller ones are all bound by the limitations of the price system, which holds them to the pursuit of a profitable price, not to the pursuit of gain in terms of material goods. Their vested rights are for the most part carried as an overhead charge in terms of price and have to be met in those terms, which will not allow an increase of net production regardless of price. The latter question will find its answer in the well-known formula of the economists, that "human wants are indefinitely extensible," particularly as regards the consumption of superfluities. The free income which is capitalized in the intangible assets of the vested interests goes to support the well-to-do investors, who are for this reason called the kept-classes, and whose keep consists in an indefinitely extensible consumption of superfluities.

6

The Divine Right of Nations

This sinister fact is patent, that the great war has arisen out of a fateful entanglement of national pretensions. And it is a fact scarcely less patent that this fateful *status quo ante* arose out of the ordinary run of that system of law and custom which has governed human intercourse among civilized nations in our time. The underlying principles of this system of law and custom have continued to govern human intercourse under a new order of material circumstances which has come into effect since these principles were first installed. These enlightened principles that go to make up the modern point of view as regards law and morals are of the eighteenth century, whereas the new order in industry is of the twentieth, and between these two dates lies an interval of unexampled change in the material conditions of life.

To all this it will be said, of course, that warfare is not a new invention, and that the national ambitions and animosities out of which wars have always arisen are of older date than the modern point of view and the machine industry; but it will also not be denied that the great war which is now coming to a provisional close is the largest and most atrocious epoch of warfare known to history, and that it has, in point of fact, arisen out of this *status quo* which has been created by these enlightened principles of the modern point of view in working out their consequences on the ground of the new order of industry.

The great war arose within that group of nations which have the full use of the industrial arts, which conduct their business and control their industries on the lines of these enlightened principles of the eighteenth century, and whose national ambitions and policies are guided by the preconceptions of national self-determination and self-assertion which these modern civilized peoples have habitually found to be good and valid. The group of belligerents has included primarily the great industrial nations, and the outcome of the war is being decided by the industrial superiority of the advanced industrial peoples. A host of slightly backward peoples—backward in the industrial respect—have been drawn into this contest of the great powers, but these have taken part only as interested outliers and as auxiliaries to be drawn on at the discretion of the chief belligerents. It has been a contest of technological superiority and industrial resources, and in the end the decision of it rests with the greater aggregation of industrial forces. Frightfulness and warlike abandon and all the beastly devices of the heathen have proved to be unavailing against the great industrial powers; partly because these things do not enduringly serve the technological needs of the contest, partly because they have run counter to that massive drift of sentiment which animates the great industrial peoples.

The center of the warlike disturbance has been the same as the center of growth and diffusion of the new order of industry. And in both respects, both as regards participation in the war and as regards their share in the new order of industry, it is not a question of geographical nearness to a geographical center, but of industrial affiliation and technological maturity. The center of disturbance and participation is a center in the technological respect; and in the end the battle goes to those few great industrial peoples who are nearest, technologically speaking, to the apex of growth of the new order. These need be superior in no other respect; the contest is decided on the merits of the industrial arts. And in this connection it may be in place to call to mind again that the state of the industrial arts is always a joint stock of knowledge and proficiency held, exercised, augmented and carried forward by the industrial community at large as a going concern. What the war has vindicated, hitherto, is the great efficiency of the mechanical industry.

But the ambitions and animosities which precipitated this contest, and which now stand ready to bring on a renewal of it in due time, are not of the industrial order, and eminently not of the new order of technology. They have been more nearly bound up with those principles of self-help that have stood over from the recent past, from the time before the new order of industry came into bearing. And there is a curious parallel between the consequences worked out by these principles in the economic system within each of these nations, on the one hand, and in the concert of nations, on the other hand. Within the nation the enlightened principles of self-help and free contract have given rise to vested interests which control the industrial system for their own use and thereby come in for a legal right to the community's net output of product over cost. Each of these vested interests habitually aims to take over as much as it can of the lucrative traffic that goes on and to get as much as it can out of the traffic, at the cost of the rest of the community. After the same analogy, and by sanction of the same liberal principles, the civilized nations, each and several, are vested with an inalienable right of "self-determination"; which being interpreted means the self-aggrandizement of each and several at the cost of the rest, by a reasonable use of force and fraud. And there has been, on the whole, no sense of shame or of moral obliquity attaching to the use of so much force and fraud as the traffic would bear, in this national enterprise of self-aggrandizement. Such has been use and wont among the civilized nations.

Meantime the new order of industry has come into bearing, with the result that any disturbance which is set afoot by any one of these self-determining nations in pursuing its own ends is sure to derange the conditions of life for all the others, just so far as these others are bound up in the same comprehensive organization of trade and industry. Full and free self-determination runs counter to the rule of Live and Let Live. After the same fashion the businesslike maneuvers of the vested interests within the nations, each managing its own affairs with an eye single to its own advantage, deranges the ordinary conditions of life for the common man, and violates the rule of Live and Let Live by that much. Self-determination, full and free, necessarily encroaches on the conditions of life for all the others.

So, just now there is talk of disallowing or abridging the inalienable right of free nations by so much as is imperatively demanded for reasonably secure conditions of life among these civilized peoples, and especially so far as is required for the orderly pursuit of profitable business by the many vested interests domiciled in these civilized countries. The project has much in com-

mon with the measures which have been entertained for the restraint of any insufferably extortionate vested interests within the
national frontiers.

In both cases alike, both in the proposed regulation of businesslike excesses at home and in the proposed league of Pacific
nations, the projected measures of sobriety and tolerance appear
to be an infraction of that inalienable right of self-direction that
makes up the substantial core of law and custom according to
the modern point of view. There is much alarm felt by the dema-
gogues at the danger which is said to threaten the national "sovereignty"; just as the vested interests are volubly apprehensive
of the "sacred rights of property." And in both cases alike the
projected measure of sobriety, tolerance and incidental infraction are designed to go no farther than is unequivocally demanded
by the imperative needs of continued life on earth; leaving the
benefit of the doubt always on the side of the insufferable vested
interests or the mischievous national ambitions, as the case may
be; and leaving the impression that it all is a concessive surrender of principles under compulsion of circumstances that will
not wait. There is also in both cases alike a well-assured likeli-
hood that the tentative revision of vested interests and of national pretensions is to be no more than an incompetent remedial
precaution, a makeshift shelter from the wrath to come.

It is evident that in both cases alike we have to do with an
incursion of ideas and considerations that are alien to the established liberal principles of human intercourse; but it is also evident that these ideas and considerations have the sanction of that
new order of things that runs in terms of tangible performance
and enforces its requisitions with cruel and unusual punishments.
It is these punishments that are to be evaded or suspended, and
immunity is sought by diplomatic measures of formality and delay rather than by tangible performance. In such a case the keepers of the established order will always look to evasion and en-
tertain a hope of avoiding casualties and holding the line by the
use of a cleverly designed masquerade.

It is the express purpose of the projected league of Pacific nations to keep the sovereign rights of national self-determination
intact for all comers; it is to be a league of nations, not a league
of peoples. But it should be sufficiently obvious, whether it is

avowed or not, that these sovereign rights can be maintained by these means only in a mutilated form. Within the framework of any such league or common understanding the nations, each and several, can continue to exercise these rights only on the basis of a mutual agreement to give up so much of their national pretensions as are patently incompatible with the common good. It involves a concessive surrender of the sovereign right of self-aggrandizement, and perhaps also an extension of the rule of Live and Let Live to cover minor nationalities within the national frontiers; a mutual agreement to play fair under the new rules that are to govern the conduct of national enterprise. Any injunction to play fair is an infraction of national sovereignty. Hitherto no liberal statesman has been so audacious as to "imagine the king's death" and lay profane hands on the divine right of nations to seek their own advantage at the cost of the rest by such means as the rule of reason shall decide to be permissible. It is only that licence is to be hedged about, and all insufferable superfluity of naughtiness is provisionally to be disallowed.

There is this evident resemblance and kinship between the vested interests of business and the sovereign rights of nations, but it does not amount to identity. There is always something more to the national sovereignty and the national pretensions; although these precautionary measures that are now under advisement as touches the legitimate bounds of both do run on singularly similar lines and are of a similarly tentative and equivocal nature. In the prudent measures by which statesmen have set themselves to curb the excesses of the greater vested interests within the nation their aim has quite consistently been to guard the free income of the lesser vested interests against the unseasonable rapacity of the greater ones; all the while that the underlying community has come into the case only as a fair field of business enterprise at large, within which there is to be maintained a reasonable degree of equal opportunity among these interests, big and little, in whom, one with another, vests the effectual usufruct of the underlying community.

It may be necessary to remark, by way of parenthesis, that while this description of these corrective measures may seem to hint at a fault, that is by no means its purpose. The fault may be there, of course, but if so it has no bearing on the argument at this point. It should also be remarked in the same connection that this description of facts does not overlook the well-conceived verbal reservations and preambles with which cautious statesmen habitually surround the common good in the face of any unseasonable rapacity on the part of the greater vested interests; it is only that the run of the facts has been quite patently to the effect so indicated. In the same connection it may also not be out of place to recall that a vested interest is a prescriptive right to get something for nothing; in which again the kinship and resemblance between vested interests in business and the sovereign rights of nations comes into view.

So, on the other hand, the great war has brought into a strong light the obvious fact that, given the existing state of the industrial arts, any unseasonable rapacity on the part of the great Powers in exercising their inalienable right of national self-determination will effectually suppress the similarly inalienable right of self-determination in any minor nationality that gets in the way. All of which is obnoxious to the liberal principle of self-help or to that of equal opportunity. Unhappily, these two guiding principles of the modern point of view—self-help and equal opportunity—have proved to be incompatible with one another under the circumstances of the new order of things. So there has come into view this project of a league, by which it is proposed to play fast and loose with the inalienable right of national self-help by setting up some sort of a collusive arrangement between the Powers, a conspiracy in restraint of national intrigue, looking to a reasonable disallowance of force and fraud in the pursuit of national ambitions.

Under the material circumstances of the new order those correctives that were once counted on to keep the run of things within the margin of tolerance have ceased to be a sufficient safeguard. By use and wont, in the Liberal scheme of statecraft as well as in the scheme of freely competitive business, implicit faith has hitherto been given to the remedial effect of punitive competition and the punitive correction of excesses by law and custom. It has been a system of adjustment by punitive afterthought. All of which may once have been well enough in its time, so long as the rate and scale of the movement of things were slow enough and small enough to be effectually overtaken and set to rights by afterthought. The modern—eighteenth-century—point of view presumes an order of things which is amenable to remedial adjustment after the event. But the new order of industry, and that sweeping equilibrium of material forces that embodies the new order, is not amenable to afterthought. Where human life and human fortunes are exposed to the swing of the machine system, or to the onset of national ambitions that are served by the machine industry, it is safety first or none. However, ripe statesmen and over-ripe captains of finance have so secure a grasp of first principles that they are still able to believe quite sincerely in the good old plan of remedial afterthought, and it still commands the affectionate service of the jurists and the diplomatic corps. Meantime the far-reaching, swift-moving, wide-sweeping machine technology has been drawn into the service of national pretensions, as well as of the vested interests that find shelter under the national pretensions, and both the remedial diplomats and the self-determination of nations are on the way to become a tale that was told.

The divine right of nations appears to be a blurred after-image of the divine rights of kings. It rests on ground more archaic and less open to scrutiny than the Natural Right of self-direction as it applies in the case of individual persons. It is a highly prized national asset, in the nature of an imponderable; and, very much as is true of the divine right of kings, any spoken doubt of its paramount validity comes near being a sin against the Holy Ghost. It cannot safely be scrutinized or defined in matter-of-fact words. As is true of the divine right of kings, so also as regards the divine right of nations, it is extremely difficult to show that it serves the common good in any material way, in any way that can be formulated or verified in terms of tangible performance. Evidently it does not come in under that mechanistic conception that rules the scheme of knowledge and belief wherever and so far as material science and the machine technology have reshaped men's habits of thought. Indeed, it is not a technological conception, late or early. It is not statable in terms of mechanical efficiency, or even in terms of price. Hence it is spoken of, often and eloquently, as being "beyond price." It is more nearly akin to magic and religion. It should perhaps best be conceived as an end in itself, or a thing-in-itself—again in close analogy with the divine right of kings. But there is no question of its substantial reality and its paramount efficacy for good and ill.

The divine—that is to say inscrutable and irresponsible—right of kings reached its best estate and put on divinity in the stirring times of the Era of State-making; when the princes and prelates "tore each other in the slime." It was of a proprietary nature, a vested interest, something in the nature of intangible assets which embodied the usufruct of the realm, including its population and resources, and which could be turned to account in the pursuit of princely or dynastic advantages at home and abroad. This divine right of princes was disallowed among the more civilized peoples on the transition to modern ways of thinking, and the sovereign rights of the prince were then taken over—at least in form and principle—by the people at large, and they have continued to be held by them as some sort of imponderable "community property,"—at least in point of form and profession. The vested interest of the prince or the dynasty in the usufruct of the underlying community is thereby presumed to have become a collective interest vested in the people of the nations and giving them a "right of user" in their own persons, knowledge, skill and resources.

The mantle of princely sovereignty has fallen on the common man—formally and according to the letter of the legal instruments. In practical effect, as "democratic sovereignty" it has been converted into a cloak to cover the nakedness of a government which does business for the kept classes. In practical effect, the shift from the dynastic politics of the era of state making to the Liberal policies based on the enlightened principles of the eighteenth century has been a shift from the pursuit of princely dominion to an imperialistic enterprise for the protection and furtherance of those vested interests that are domiciled within the national frontiers. That such has been the practical outcome is due to the fact that these enlightened principles of the eighteenth century comprise as their chief article the "natural," right of ownership. The later course of events has decided that the ownership of property in sufficiently large blocks will control the country's industrial system and thereby take over the disposal of the community's net output of product over cost; on which the vested interests live and on which, therefore, the kept classes feed. Hence the chief concern of those gentlemanly national governments that have displaced the dynastic states is always and consistently the maintenance of the rights of ownership and investment.

However, these pecuniary interests of investment and free income are not all that is covered by the mantle of democratic sovereignty. Nor will it hold true that the common man has no share in the legacy of sovereignty and national enterprise which the enlightened democratic commonwealth has taken over from the departed dynastic regime. The divine right of the prince included certain imponderables, as well as the usufruct of the material resources of the realm. There were the princely dignity and honor, which were no less substantial an object of value and ambition and were no less tenaciously held by the princes of the dynastic regime than the revenues and material "sinews of war" on which the prestige and honor rested. And the common man of the democratic commonwealth has at least come in for a ratable share in these imponderables of prestige and honor that so are comprised under the divine right of the nation. He has an undivided interest in the glamour of national achievement, and he can swell with just pride in contemplating the triumphs of his gentlemanly government over the vested interests domiciled in any foreign land, or with just indignation at any diplomatic setback suffered by the vested interests domiciled in his own.

There is also a more tangible, though more petty, advantage gained for the common man in having formally taken over the sovereignty from the dead hand of the dynastic prince. The common man being now vested with the divine right of national sovereignty, held in undivided community ownership, it is ceremonially necessary for the gentlemanly stewards of the kept classes to consult the wishes of this their sovereign on any matters of policy that cannot wholly be carried through in a diplomatic corner and under cover of night and cloud. He, collectively, holds an eventual power of veto. And this power of veto has in practice been found to be something of a safeguard against any universal and enduring increase of hardship at the hands of the gentlemen-investors to whom the conduct of the nation's affairs has been "entrusted;" a very modest safeguard, it is true, but always of some eventual consequence. There is the difference that in the democratic commonwealth the common man has to be managed rather than driven—except for minor groups of common men who live on the lower-common levels, and except for recurrent periods of legislative hysteria and judiciary blind-staggers. And it is pleasanter to be managed than to be driven. Chicane is a more humane art than corporal punishment. Imperial England is, after all, a mild-mannered stepmother than Imperial Germany.

And always the common man comes in for his ratable share in the glamour of national achievement, in war and peace; and this imponderable gain of the spirit is also something. The value of these collective imponderables of national prestige and collective honor is not to be made light of. These count for very much in the drift and set of national sentiment, and moral issues of national moment are wont to arise out of them. Indeed, they constitute the chief incentive which holds the common man to an unrepining constancy in the service of the "national interests." So that, while the tangible shell of material gain appears to have fallen to the democratic community's kept classes, yet the "psychic income" that springs from national enterprise, the spiritual kernel of national elation they share with the common man on an equitable footing of community interest.

The vested rights of the nation are of the essence of that order of things which enjoys the unqualified sanction of the modern point of view. Like any other vested interest, these rights are conceived in other terms than those which are native to the new order of material science and technology. They are of an older and more spiritual order, so far as regards the principles of knowledge and belief on which they rest. But whatever may be their remoter pedigree, they have the sanction of that body of principles that is called the modern point of view, and they belong in the scheme of things handed on by the Liberal movement of the eighteenth and nineteenth century. Apart from the imponderable values which fall under the head of national prestige, these vested rights of the nation can be defined as an extension to the commonwealth of the same natural rights of self-direction and personal security—free contract and self-help—that are secured to the individual citizen under the common law.

Yet, while the national policies of the democratic commonwealths are managed by Liberal statesmen in behalf of the vested interests, they still run on the ancient lines of dynastic statecraft, as worked out by the statesmen of the ancient regime; and the common man is still passably content to see the traffic run along on those lines. The things which are considered desirable to be done in the way of national enterprise, as well as the sufficient reasons for doing them, still have much of the medieval color. National pretensions, enterprise, rivalry, intrigue and dissensions among the democratic commonwealths are still such as would have been intelligible to Macchiavelli, Frederick the Great, Metternich, Bismarck, or the Elder Statesmen of Japan. Diplomatic intercourse still runs in the same terms of systematized prevarication, and still turns about the same schedule of national pretensions that contented the medieval spirit of these masters of dynastic intrigue. As a matter of course and of common sense the nations still conceive themselves to be rivals, whose national interests are incompatible, and whose divine right it is to gain something at one another's cost, after the fashion of rival bandits or business concerns. They still seek dominion and still conceive themselves to have extra-territorial interests of a proprietary sort. They still hold and still seek vested rights in colonial possessions and in extra-territorial priorities and concessions of diverse and dubious kinds. There still are conferences, stipulations and guarantees between the Powers, touching the "Open Door" in China, or the equitable partition of Africa, which read like a chapter on Honor among Thieves.

All this run of national pretensions, wrangles, dominion, aggrandizement, chicane, and ill-will, is nothing more than the old familiar trading stock of the diplomatic brokers who do business in dynastic force and fraud—also called *Realpolitik*. The democratic nations have taken over in bulk the whole job-lot of vested interests and divine rights that once made the monarch of the old order an unfailing source of outrage and desolation. In the hands of those "Elder Statesmen" who once did business under the signature of the dynasty, the traffic in statecraft yielded nothing better than a mess of superfluous affliction; there is no reason to apprehend that a continuation of the same traffic under the management of the younger statesmen who now do business in the name of the democratic commonwealth is likely to bring anything more comfortable, even though the legal instruments in the case may carry the rubber-stamp O.K. of the common man. The same items will foot up to the same sum; and in either case the net gain is always something appreciably less than nothing.

These national interests are part of the medieval system of ends, ways and means, as it stood, complete and useless, at that juncture when the democratic commonwealth took over the divine rights of the crown. It should not be extremely difficult to understand why they have stood over, or why they still command the dutiful approval of the common man. It is a case of aimless survival, on the whole, due partly to the inertia of habit and tradition, partly to the solicitous advocacy of these assumed national interests by those classes—the trading and office-holding classes—who stand to gain something by the pursuit of them at the cost of the rest. By tenacious tradition out of the barbarian past these peoples have continued to be rival nations living in a state of habitual enmity and distrust, for no better reason than that they have not taken thought and changed their mind.

After some slackening of national animosities and some disposition to neglect national pretensions during the earlier decades of the great era of Liberalism, the democratic nations have been gradually shifting back to a more truculent attitude and a more crafty and more rapacious management in all international relations. This aggressive chauvinistic policy has been called Imperialism. The movement has visibly kept pace, more or less closely, with the increasing range and volume of commerce and foreign investments during the same period. And to further this business enterprise there has been an ever-increasing resort to military power. It is reasonably believed that traders and investors in foreign parts are able to derive a larger profit from their business when they have the backing of a powerful and aggressive national government; particularly in their dealings with helpless and backward peoples, and more particularly if their own national government is sufficiently unscrupulous and overbearing, — which may confidently be counted on so long as these governments continue to be administered by the gentlemanly delegates of the vested interests and the kept classes.

As regards the intrinsic value which is popularly attached to the imponderable national possessions, in the way of honor and prestige, there is little to be said, beyond the stale reflection that there is no disputing about tastes. It all is at least a profitable illusion, for the use of those who are in a position to profit by it. Such as the crown and the officeholders. But the people of the civilized nations believe themselves to have also a material interest of some sort in enlarging the national dominions and in extending the foreign trade of their businessmen and safeguarding the foreign claims of their vested interests. And the Americans, like many others, harbor the singular delusion that they can derive a collective benefit from obstructing the country's trade at the national frontiers by means of a tariff barrier, and so defeating their own industry by that much. It is a survival out of the barbarian past, out of the time when the dynastic politicians were occupied with isolating the nation and making it self-sufficient, as an engine of warlike enterprise for the pursuit of dynastic ambitions and the greater discomfort of their neighbors. In an increasing degree as the new order of industry has come into bearing, any such policy of industrial isolation and self-sufficiency has become more difficult and more injurious; for a free range and unhindered specialization is of the essence of the new industrial order.

The experience of the war has shown conclusively that no one country can hereafter supply its own needs either in raw materials or in finished goods. Both the winning and the losing side have shown that. The new industrial order necessarily overlaps the national frontiers, even in the case of a nation possessed of so extensive and varied natural resources as America. So that in spite of all the singularly ingenious obstruction of the American tariff the Americans still continue to draw on foreign sources for most or all of their tea, coffee, sugar, tropical and semi-tropical fruits, vegetable oils, vegetable gums and pigments, cordage fibers, silks, rubber, and a bewildering multitude of minor articles of daily use. Even so peculiarly American an industry as chewing gum is wholly dependent on foreign raw material, and quite unavoidably so. The most that can be accomplished by any tariff under these circumstances is more or less obstruction. Isolation and self-sufficiency are already far out of the question.

But there are certain vested interests which find their profit in maintaining a tariff barrier as a means of keeping the price up and keeping the supply down; and the common man still faithfully believes that the profits which these vested interests derive in this way from increasing the cost of his livelihood and decreasing the net productivity of his industry will benefit him in some mysterious way. He is persuaded that high prices and a scant supply of goods at a high labor cost is a desirable state of things. This is incredible, but there is no denying the fact. He knows, of course, that the profits of business go to the business-men, the vested interests, and to no one else; but he is still beset with the picturesque hallucination that any unearned income which goes to those vested interests whose central office is in New Jersey is paid to himself in some underhand way, while the gains of those vested interests that are domiciled in Canada are obviously a grievous net loss to him. The tariff moves in a mys-terious way, its wonders to perform.

To all adult persons of sound mind, and not unduly clouded with the superstitions of the price system, it is an obvious matter of fact that any protective tariff is an obstruction to industry and a means of impoverishment, just so far as it is effective. The arguments to the contrary invariably turn out to be pettifogger's special pleading for some vested interest or for a warlike na-tional policy, and these arguments convince only those persons who are able to believe that a part is greater than the whole. It also lies in the nature of protective tariffs that they always cost the nation disproportionately much more than they are worth to those vested interests which profit by them. In this respect they are like any other method of businesslike sabotage. Their aim, and presumably their effect is to keep the price up by keeping the supply down, to hinder competitors and retard production. As in other instances of businesslike sabotage, therefore, the net margin of advantage to those who profit by it is greatly less than what it costs the community.

Yet it is to be noted that the Americans have prospered, on the whole, under protective tariffs which have been as ingeniously and comprehensively foolish as could well be contrived. There is even some color of reason in the contentions of the protection-ists that the more reasonable tariffs have commonly been more depressing to industry than the most imbecile of them. All of which should be disquieting to the advocates of free trade. The defect of the free-trade argument, and the disappointment of free-trade policies, lies in overlooking the fact that in the absence of an obstructive tariff substantially the same amount of obstruc-tion has to be accomplished by other means, if business is to prosper. And business prosperity is the only manner of prosperity known or provided for among the civilized nations. It is the only manner of prosperity on which the divine right of the nation gives it a claim. A protective tariff is only an alternative method of businesslike sabotage. If and so far as this method of keeping the supply of goods within salutary bounds is not resorted to, other means of accomplishing the same result must be employed. For so long as investment continues to control industry the welfare of the community is bound up with the prosperity of its business; and business cannot be carried on without reasonably profitable prices; and reasonably profitable prices cannot be maintained without a salutary limitation of the supply; which means slowing down production to such a rate and volume as the traffic will bear.

A protective tariff is only one means of crippling the country's industrial forces, for the good of business. In its absence all that matter will be taken care of by other means. The tariff may perhaps be a little the most flagrant method of sabotage by which the vested interests are enabled to do a reasonably profitable business; but there is nothing more than a difference of degree, and not a large difference at that. So long as industry is managed with a view to a profitable price it is quite indispensable to guard against an excessive rate and volume of output. In the absence of all businesslike sabotage the productive capacity of the industrial system would very shortly pass all reasonable bounds, prices would decline disastrously and overhead charges would not be covered, fixed charges on corporation securities and other credit instruments could not be met, and the whole structure of business enterprise would collapse, as it occasionally has done in times of "over-production." There is no doing business without a fair price, since the net price over cost is the motive of business. A protective tariff is, in effect, an auxiliary safeguard against overproduction. Incidentally the fact that its imposition does not result in insufferable hardship serves also to show that the new order of industry is highly productive, quite inordinately productive in fact. And it is a divine right of the nation to use its discretion and offset this inordinate efficiency of its common stock of knowledge by adroitly crippling its own commerce and the commerce of its neighbors, for the benefit of those vested interests that are domiciled within the national frontiers.

But the divine right of national self-direction also covers much else of the same description, besides the privilege of setting up a tariff in restraint of trade. There are many channels of such discrimination, of diverse kinds, but always it will be found that these channels are channels of sabotage and that they serve the advantage of some group of vested interests which do business under the shelter of the national pretensions. There are foreign investments and concessions to be procured and safeguarded for the nation's businessmen by moral persuasion backed with warlike force, and the common man pays the cost; there is discrimination to be exercised and perhaps subsidies and credits to be accorded those of the nation's businessmen who derive a profit from shipping, for the discomfiture of alien competitors, and the common man pays the cost; there are colonies to be procured and administered at the public expense for the private gain of certain traders, concessionaires and administrative office-holders, and the common man pays the cost. Back of it all is the nation's divine right to carry arms, to support a competitive military and naval establishment, which has ceased, under the new order, to have any other material use than to enforce or defend the businesslike right of particular vested interests to get something for nothing in some particular place and in some particular way, and the common man pays the cost and swells with pride.

7

Live and Let Live

The Nation's inalienable right of self-direction and self-help is of the same nature and derivation as the like inalienable right of self-help vested in an irresponsible king by the grace of God. In both cases alike it is a divine right, in the sense that it is irresponsible and will not bear scrutiny, being an arbitrary right of self-help at the cost of any whom it may concern. There is the further parallel that in both cases alike the ordinary exercise of these rights confers no material benefit on the underlying community. In practical effect the exercise of such divine rights, whether by a sovereign monarch or by the officials of a sovereign nation, works damage and discomfort to one and another, within the national frontiers or beyond them, with nothing better to show for it than some relatively slight gain in prestige or in wealth for some relatively small group of privileged persons or vested interests. And the gain of those who profit by this means is always got at the cost of the common man at home and abroad. These inalienable rights are an abundant source of grievances to be redressed at the cost of the common man.

It has long been a stale commonplace that the quarrels of competitive kings in pursuit of their divine rights have brought nothing but damage and discomfort to the underlying peoples whose material wealth and man power have been made use of for national enterprise of this kind. And it is no less evident, though perhaps less notorious, that the pursuit of national advantages by competitive nations by use of the same material wealth and man power unavoidably brings nothing better than the same net output of damage and discomfort to all the peoples concerned. There is of course the reservation that in the one case the kings and their accomplices and pensioners have come in for some gain in prestige and in perquisites, while in the case of the competitive nations certain vested interests and certain groups of the kept classes stand to gain something in the way of perquisites and free income; but always and in the nature of the case the total gain is less than the cost; and always the gain goes to the kept classes and the cost falls on the common man. So much is notorious, particularly so far as it is a question of material gain and loss. So far as it is an immaterial question of jealousy and prestige, the line of division runs between nations, but as regards material gain and loss it is always a division between the kept classes and the common man; and always the common man has more to lose than the kept classes stand to gain.

The war is now concluded, provisionally, and peace is in prospect for the immediate future, also provisionally. As is true between individuals, so also among the nations, peace means the same thing as Live and Let Live, which also means the same thing as a world made safe for democracy. And the rule of Live and Let Live means the discontinuance of animosity and discrimination between the nations. Therefore it involves the disallowance of such incompatible national pretensions as are likely to afford ground for international grievances—which comes near involving the disallowance of all those claims and perquisites that habitually go in under the captions of "national self-determination" and "national integrity," as these phrases are employed in diplomatic intercourse. At the same time it involves the disallowance of all those class pretensions and vested interests that make for dissension within the nation. Ill will is not a practicable basis of peace, whether within the nation or between the nations. So much is plain matter of course. What may be the chances of peace and war, at home and abroad, in the light of these blunt and obvious principles taken in conjunction with the diplomatic negotiations now going forward at home and abroad, all that is sufficiently perplexing.

At home in America for the transient time being, the war administration has under pressure of necessity somewhat loosened the stranglehold of the vested interests on the country's industry; and in so doing it has shocked the safe and sane businessmen into a state of indignant trepidation and has at the same time doubled the country's industrial output. But all that has avowedly been only for the transient time being, "for the period of the war," as a distasteful concession to demands that would not wait. So that the country now faces a return to the precarious conditions of a provisional peace on the lines of the *status quo ante.* Already the vested interests are again tightening their hold and are busily arranging for a return to business as usual; which means working at cross-purposes as usual, waste of work and materials as usual, restriction of output as usual, unemployment as usual, labor quarrels as usual, competitive selling as usual, mendacious advertising as usual, waste of superfluities as usual by the kept classes, and privation as usual for the common man. All of which may conceivably be put up with by this people "lest a worse evil befall." All this runs blamelessly in under the rule of Live and Let Live as interpreted in the light of those enlightened principles of self-help that have come down from the eighteenth century and that go to make up the established scheme of law and order, although it does not meet the needs of the same rule as it would be enforced by the exigencies of the new order in industry.

Meanwhile, abroad, the gentlemen of the old school who direct the affairs of the nations are laying down the lines on which peace is to be established and maintained, with a painstaking regard for all those national pretensions and discriminations that have always made for international embroilment, and with an equally painstaking disregard for all those exigencies of the new order that call for a *de facto* observance of the rule of Live and Let Live. It is notorious beyond need of specification that the new order in industry, even more insistently than any industrial situation that has gone before, calls for a wide and free intercourse in trade and industry, regardless of national frontiers and national jealousies. In this connection a national frontier, as it is commonly made use of in current statecraft, is a line of demarcation for working at cross purposes, for mutual obstruction and distrust. It is only necessary to recall that the erection of a new national frontier across any community which has previously enjoyed the privilege of free intercourse unburdened with customs frontiers will be felt to be a grievous burden; and that the erection of such a line of demarcation for other diplomatic work at mutual cross-purposes is likewise an unmistakable nuisance.

Yet, in the peace negotiations now going forward the gentlemen of the old school to whom the affairs of the nations have
been "entrusted"—by shrewd management on their own part—
continue to safeguard all this apparatus of mutual defeat and distrust, —and indeed this is the chief or sole object of their solici-
tude, as it also is the chief or sole object of those vested interests
for whose benefit the diplomatic gentlemen of the old school
continue to manage the affairs of the nations.

The state of the case is plainly to be seen in the proposals of
those nationalities that are now coming forward with a new claim
to national self-determination. Invariably any examination of the
bill of particulars set up by the spokesmen of these proposed
new national establishments will show that the material point of
it all is an endeavor to set up a national apparatus for working at
mutual cross purposes with their neighbors, to add something to
the waste and confusion caused by the national discriminations
already in force, to violate the rule of Live and Let Live at some
new point and by some further apparatus of discomfort.

There are nationalities that get along well enough, to all appearance, without being "nations" in that militant and obstructive fashion that is aimed at in these projected creations of the
diplomatic nation makers. Such are the Welsh and the Scottish,
for instance. But it is not the object lesson of Welsh or Scottish
experience that guides the new projects. The nationalities which
are now escaping from a rapacious Imperialism of the old order
are being organized and managed by the safe and sane gentlemen of the old school, who have got their notions of safety and
sanity from the diplomatic intrigue of that outworn imperialism
out of which these oppressed nationalities aim to escape. And
these gentlemen of the old school are making no move in the
direction of tolerance and good will—as how should they when
all their conceptions of what is right and expedient are the diplomatic preconceptions of the old regime. They, being gentlemen
of the old school, will have none of that amicable and unassuming nationality which contents the Welsh and the Scottish who
have tried out this matter and have in the end come to hold fast
only so much of their national pretensions as will do no material
harm. What is aimed at is not a disallowance of bootless national
jealousies, but only a shift from an intolerable imperialism on a

large scale to an *ersatz*-imperialism drawn on a smaller scale, conducted on the same general lines of competitive diplomacy and serving interests of the same general kind—vested interests of business or of privilege.

The projected new nations are not patterned on the Welsh or the Scottish model, but for all that there is nothing novel in their design; and how should there be when they are the offspring of the imagination of these safe and sane gentlemen of the old school fertilized with the ancient conceptions of imperialistic diplomacy and national prestige. In effect it is all drawn to the scale and pattern already made notorious by the Balkan states. It should also be safe to presume that the place and value of these newly emerging nations in the comity of peoples under the prospective regime of provisional peace will be something not notably different from what the Balkan states have habitually placed on view; which may be deprecated by many well-meaning persons, but which is scarcely to be undone by well-wishing. The chances of war and politics have thrown the fortunes of these projected new nations into the hands of these politic gentlemen of the old school, and by force of inveterate habit these very practical persons are unable to conceive that anything else than a Balkan state is fit to take the place of that imperial rule that has now fallen into decay. So Balkan-state national establishments appear to be the best there is in prospect in the new world of safe democracy.

So true is this, that even in those instances, such as the Finns and other fragments of the Russian imperial dominions, where a newly emerging nation has set out to go on its way without taking pains to safeguard the grievances of the old order, —even in these instances that should seem to concern no one but themselves, the gentlemen of the old school who guard the political institutions of the old order in the world at large find it impossible to keep their hands off and to let these adventurous pilgrims of hope go about their own business in their own way. Self-determination proves to be insufferable if it partakes of the new order rather than of the old, at least so long as the safe and sane gentlemen of the old school can hinder it by any means at their command. It is felt that the vested interests, which underlie the gentlemen of the old school, would not be sufficiently secure in the keeping of these unshorn and unshaven pilgrims of hope, and the doubt may be well taken. So that, within the intellectual horizon of the practical statesmen, the only safe, sane, and profitable manner of national establishment and national policy for these newcomers is something after the familiar fashion of the Balkan states; and it may also be admitted quite broadly that these newly arriving peoples commonly are content to seek their national fortunes along precisely these Balkan state lines; although the Finns and their like are perhaps to be counted as an unruly exception to the rule.

These Balkan states, whose spirit, aims, and ways are so admirable in the eyes of the gentlemanly keepers of the old political and economic order, are simply a case of imperialism in the raw. They are all and several still in the pickpocket stage of dynastic statemaking, comparable with the state of Prussia before Frederick the Great Pickpocket came to the throne. And now, with much sage counsel from the safe and sane statesmen of the *status quo ante,* Czechs, Slovaks, Slovenes, Ruthenians, Ukrainians, Croats, and the Polish peoples are breathlessly elbowing their way into line with these minuscular Machiavellians. Quite unchastened by their age-long experience in adversity they are all alike clamoring for national establishments stocked up with all the time-tried contrivances for discomfort and defeat. With one hand they are making frantic gestures of distress for an "outlet to the sea" by means of which to escape insufferable obstruction of their overseas trade by their nationally minded neighbors, while with the other hand they are feverishly at work to contrive a customs frontier of their own, together with other standard devices for obstructing their neighbors' trade and their own, so soon as they shall have any trade to obstruct. Such is the force of habit and tradition. In other words, these peoples are aiming to become self-determining nations in good standing.

And all the while it is plain to all men that a national "outlet to the sea" has no meaning in time of peace and in the absence of national governments working at cross-purposes. Which comes near to saying that the sole material object of these new projects in nation making is to work at cross-purposes with their neighbors across the newfound national frontiers. So also it is plain that this mutual working at cross-purposes between the nations hinders the keeping of the peace, even when it is all mitigated with all the approved apparatus of diplomatic make-believe, compromise, and intrigue. Just as it is plain that the peace is not to be kept by use of armaments, but all the while national armaments are also included as an indispensable adjunct of national life, in all the projects of these new nations of the Balkan pattern. The right to carry arms is an inalienable right of national self-determination and an indispensable means of self-help, as understood by these nation makers of the old school. So also it is plain that national pretensions in the field of foreign trade and investment, and all the diversified expedients for furthering and protecting the profitable enterprise of the vested interests in foreign parts, run consistently at cross-purposes with the keeping of the peace.

And all the while the rule of Live and Let Live, as it works out within the framework of the new industrial order, will not tolerate these things. But the rule of Live and Let Live, which embodies the world's hope of peace on earth and a practicable modicum of good will among men, is not of the essence of that time-worn statesmanship which is now busily making the world safe for the vested interests. Neglect and disallowance of those things that make for embroilment does not enter into the counsels of the nation-makers or of those stupendous figures of veiled statecraft that now move in the background and are shaping the destinies of these and other nations with a view to the *status quo ante.*

All these peoples that now hope to be nations have long been nationalities. A nation is an organization for collective offense and defense, in peace and war, —essentially based on hate and fear of other nations; a nationality is a cultural group, bound together by home-bred affinities of language, tradition, use and wont, and commonly also by a supposed community race, — essentially based on sympathies and sentiments of self-complacency within itself. The Welsh and the Scottish are nationalities, more or less well defined, although they are not nations in the ordinary meaning of the word; so also are the Irish, with a difference, and such others as the Finns and the Armenians. The American republic is a nation, but not a nationality in any full measure. The Welsh and the Scottish have learned the wisdom of Live and Let Live, within the peace of the Empire, and they are not moving to break bounds and set up a national integrity after the Balkan pattern.

The case of the Irish is peculiar; at least so they say. They, that is to say the Irish by sentiment rather than by domicile, the Irish people as contrasted with the vested interests of Ulster, of the landlords, of the Church, and of the bureaucracy, — these Irish have long been a nationality and are now mobilizing all their force to set up a Balkan state, autonomous and defensible, within the formal bounds of the Empire or without. Their case is peculiar and instructive. It throws a light on the margin of tolerance, of what the traffic will bear, beyond which an increased pressure on a subject population will bring no added profit to the vested interests for whose benefit the pressure is brought to bear. It is a case of the Common Man hard ridden in due legal form by the vested interests of the Island, and of the neighboring island, which are duly backed by an alien and biased bureaucracy aided and abetted by the priestly pickpockets of the poor. So caught in this way between the devil and the deep sea, it is small wonder if they have chosen in the end to follow counsels of desperation and are moving to throw their lot into the deep sea of national self-help and international intrigue. They have reached the point where they have ceased to say: "It might have been worse." The case of the Finns, Jews, and Armenians is not greatly different in general effect.

It is easy to fall into a state of perturbation about the evil case of the submerged, exploited, and oppressed minor nationalities; and it is not unusual to jump to the conclusion that national self-determination will surely mend their evil case. National self-determination and national integrity are words to conjure with, and there is no denying that very substantial results have been known to follow from such conjuring. But self-determination is not a sovereign remedy, particularly not as regards the material conditions of life for the common man, for that somewhat more than nine-tenths of the population who always finally have to bear the cost of any national establishment. It has been tried, and the point is left in doubt. So the case of Belgium or of Serbia during the past four years has been scarcely less evil than that of the Armenians or the Poles. Belgium and Serbia were nations, in due form, very much after the pattern aimed at in the new projected nations already spoken of, whereas the Armenians and the Poles have been subject minor nationalities. Belgium, Serbia, and Poland have been subject to the ravages of an imperial power which claims rank as a civilized people, whereas the Armenians have been manhandled by the Turks. So, again, the Irish are a subject minor nationality, whereas the Romanians are a nation in due form. In fact the Romanians are just such a Balkan state as the Irish aspire to become. But no doubt the common man is appreciably worse off in his material circumstances in Romania than in Ireland. Japan, too, is not only a self-determining nation with a full charge of national integrity, but it is a Great Power; yet the common man—the somewhat more than nine-tenths of the population—is doubtless worse off in point of hard usage and privation in Japan than in Ireland.

In further illustration of this doubt and perplexity with regard to the material value of national self-determination, the case of the three Scandinavian countries may be worth citing. They are all and several self-determining nations, in that Pickwickian sense in which any country which is not a Great Power may be self-determining in the twentieth century. But they differ in size, population, wealth, power, and political consequence. In these respects the sequence runs: Sweden, Denmark, Norway, the latter being the smallest, poorest, least self-determining, and in point of self-determining nationalism altogether the most spectacularly foolish of the lot. But so far as concerns the material conditions of life for the common man, they are unmistakably the most favorable, or the most nearly tolerable, in Norway, and the least so in Sweden. The upshot of evidence from these, and from other instances that might be cited, is to leave the point in doubt. It is not evident that the common man has anything to gain by national self-determination, so far as regards his material conditions of life; nor does it appear, on the evidence of these instances, that he has much to lose by that means.

These Scandinavians differ from the Balkan states in that they perforce have no imperialistic ambitions. There may of course be a question on this head so far as concerns the frame of mind of the royal establishment in the greater one of the Scandinavian kingdoms; there is not much that is worth saying about that matter, and the less that is said, the less annoyance. It is a matter of no significance, anyway. The Scandinavians are in effect not imperialistic, perforce. Which means that in their international relations they formally adhere to the rule of Live and Let Live. Not so in their domestic policy, however. They have all endowed themselves with all the encumbrances of national pretensions and discrimination which their circumstances will admit. Apart from a court and church which foot up to nothing more comfortable than a gratuitous bill of expense, they are also content to carry the burden of a national armament, a protective tariff, a national consular service, and a diplomatic service which takes care of a moderately burdensome series of treaty agreements governing the trade relations of the Scandinavian business community; all designed for the benefit of the vested interests and the kept classes of the nation, and all at the cost of the common man.

The case of these relatively free, relatively unassuming, and relatively equitable national establishments is also instructive. They come as near the rule of Live and Let Live as any national establishment well can and still remain a national establishment actuated by notions of competitive self-help. But all the while the national administration runs along, with nothing better to show to any impartial scrutiny than a considerable fiscal burden and a moderate volume of hindrance to the country's industry, together with some incidental benefit to the vested interests and the kept classes at the cost of the underlying community. These Scandinavians occupy a peculiar position in the industrial world. They are each and several too small to make up anything like a self-contained industrial community, even under the most unreserved pressure of national exclusiveness. Their industries necessarily are part and parcel of the industrial system at large, with which they are bound in relations of give and take at every point. Yet they are content to carry a customs tariff of fairly grotesque dimensions and a national consular service of more grotesque dimensions still. This situation is heightened by their relatively sterile soil, their somewhat special and narrow range of natural resources, and their high latitude, which precludes any home growth of many of the indispensable materials of industry under the new order. Yet they are content to carry their customs tariff, their special commercial treaties, and their consular service—for the benefit of their vested interests.

It should seem that this elaborate superfluity of national outlay and obstruction should work great hardship to the underlying community whose industry is called on to carry this burden of lag, leak, and friction. And doubtless the burden is sufficiently real. It amounts, of course, to the nation's working at cross-purposes with itself, for the benefit of those special interests that stand to gain a little something by it all. But in this as in other works of sabotage there are compensating effects, and these should not be overlooked; particularly since the case is fairly typical of what commonly happens. The waste and sabotage of the national establishment and its obstructive policy works no intolerable hardship, because it all runs its course and eats its fill within that margin of sabotage and wasteful consumption that would have to be taken care of by some other agency in the absence of this one. That is to say, something like the same volume of sabotage and waste is indispensable to the prosperity of business under the conditions of the new order, so long as business and industry are managed under the conditions imposed by the price system. By one means or another prices must be maintained at a profitable level for reasons of business; therefore the output must be restricted to a reasonable rate and volume, and wasteful consumption must be provided for, on pain of a failing market. And all this may as well be taken care of by use of a princely court, an otiose church, a picturesque army, a well-fed diplomatic and consular service, and a customs frontier. In the absence of all this national apparatus of sabotage substantially the same results would have to be got at by the less seemly means of a furtive conspiracy in restraint of trade among the vested interests. There is always something to be said for the national integrity.

The case of these Scandinavian nations, taken in connection and comparison with what is to be seen elsewhere, appears to say that a national establishment which has no pretensions to power and no imperialistic ambitions is preferable, in point of economy and peaceable behavior, to an establishment which carries these attributes of self-determination and self-help. The more nearly the national integrity and self-determination approaches to make-believe the less mischief is it likely to work at home and the more nearly will it be compatible with the rule of Live and Let Live in dealing with its neighbors. And the further implication is plain without argument, that the most beneficent change that can conceivably overtake any national establishment would be to let it fall into "innocuous disuse." Apparently, the less of it the better, with no apparent limit short of the vanishing point.

Such appears to be the object lesson enforced by recent and current events, in so far as concerns the material fortunes of the underlying community at large as well as the keeping of the peace. But it does not therefore follow that all men and classes will have the same interest in so neutralizing the nation's powers and disallowing the national pretensions. The existing nations are not of a homogeneous make-up within themselves—perhaps less so in proportion as they have progressively come under the rule of the new order in industry and in business. There is an increasingly evident cleavage of interest between industry and business, or between production and ownership, or between tangible performance and free income, —one phrase may serve as well as another, and neither is quite satisfactory to mark the contrast of interest between the common man on the one hand and the vested interests and kept classes on the other hand. But it should be sufficiently plain that the national establishment and its control of affairs has a value for the vested interests different from what it has for the underlying community.

Quite plainly the new order in industry has no use or place for national discrimination or national pretensions of any kind; and quite plainly such a phrase as "national integrity" has no shadow of meaning for this new industrial order which overruns national frontiers and overcomes national discrimination as best it can, in all directions and all the time. For industry as carried on under the new order, the overcoming of national discrimination is part of the ordinary day's work. But it is otherwise with the new order of business enterprise, —large scale, corporate, resting on intangible assets, and turning on free income which flows from managerial sabotage. The business community has urgent need of an efficient national establishment both at home and abroad. A settled government, duly equipped with national pretensions, and with legal and military power to maintain the sacredness of contracts at home and to enforce the claims of its businessmen abroad, —such an establishment is invaluable for the conduct of business, though its industrial value may not unusually be less than nothing.

Industry is a matter of tangible performance in the way of producing goods and services. And in this connection it is well to recall that a vested interest is a prescriptive right to get something for nothing. Now, any project of reconstruction, the scope and method of which are governed by considerations of tangible performance, is likely to allow only a subsidiary consideration or something less to the legitimate claims of the vested interests, whether they are vested interests of business or of privilege. It is more than probable that in such a case national pretensions in the way of preferential concessions in commerce and investment will be allowed to fall into neglect, so far as to lose all value to any vested interest whose fortunes they touch. These things have no effect in the way of net tangible performance. They only afford ground for preferential pecuniary rights, always at the cost of someone else; but they are of the essence of things in that pecuniary order within which the vested interests of business live and move. So also such a matter-of-fact project of reconstruction will be likely materially to revise outstanding credit obligations, including corporation securities, or perhaps even bluntly to disallow claims of this character to free income on the part of beneficiaries who can show no claim on grounds of current tangible performance. All of which is inimical to the best good of the vested interests and the kept classes.

Reconstruction which partakes of this character in any sensible degree will necessarily be viewed with the liveliest apprehension by the gentlemanly statesmen of the old school, by the kept classes, and by the captains of finance. It will be deplored as a subversion of the economic order, a destruction of the country's wealth, a disorganization of industry, and a sure way to poverty, bloodshed, and pestilence. In point of fact, of course, what such a project may be counted on to subvert is that dominion of ownership by which the vested interests control and retard the rate and volume of production. The destruction of wealth in such a case will touch, directly, only the value of the securities, not the material objects to which these securities have given title of ownership; it would be a disallowance of ownership, not a destruction of useful goods. Nor need any disorganization or disability of productive industry follow from such a move; indeed, the apprehended cancelment of the claims to income covered by negotiable securities would by that much cancel the fixed over-head charges resting on industrial enterprise, and so further pro-duction by that much. But for those persons and classes whose keep is drawn from prescriptive rights of ownership or of privi-lege the consequences of such a shifting of ground from vested interest to tangible performance would doubtless be deplorable. In short, "Bolshevism is a menace"; and the wayfaring man out of Armenia will be likely to ask: A menace to whom?

8

The Vested Interests and the Common Man

In the eighteenth century certain principles of enlightened common sense were thrown into formal shape and adopted by the civilized peoples of that time to govern the system of law and order, use and want, under which they chose to live. So far as concerns economic relations the principles which so became incorporated into the system of civilized law and custom at that time were the principles of equal opportunity, self-determination, and self-help. Chief among the specific rights by which this civilized scheme of equal opportunity and self-help were to be safeguarded were the rights of free contract and security of property. These make up the substantial core of that system of principles which is called the modern point of view, in so far as concerns trade, industry, investment, credit obligations, and whatever else may properly be spoken of as economic institutions. And these still stand over today, paramount among the inalienable rights of all free citizens in all free countries; they are the groundwork of the economic system as it runs today, and this existing system can undergo no material change of character so long as these paramount rights of civilized men continue to be inalienable. Any move to set these rights aside would be subversive of the modern economic order; whereas no revision or alteration of established rights and usages will amount to a revolutionary move, so long as it does not disallow these paramount economic rights.

When the constituent principles of the modern point of view were accepted and the modern scheme of civilized life was therewith endorsed by the civilized peoples, in the eighteenth century, these rights of self-direction and self-help were counted on as the particular and sufficient safeguard of equity and industry in any civilized country. They were counted on to establish equal-

ity among men in all their economic relations and to maintain
the industrial system at the highest practicable degree of productive efficiency. They were counted on to give enduring effect to
the rule of Live and Let Live. And such is still the value ascribed
to these rights in the esteem of modern men. The maintenance of
law and order still means primarily and chiefly the maintenance
of these rights of ownership and pecuniary obligation.

But things have changed since that time in such a way that the
rule of Live and Let Live is no longer completely safeguarded
by maintaining these rights in the shape given them in the eighteenth century, —or at least there are large sections of the people
in these civilized countries who are beginning to think so, which
is just as good for practical purposes. Things have changed in
such a way since that time, that the ownership of property in
large holdings now controls the nation's industry, and therefore
it controls the conditions of life for those who are or wish to be
engaged in industry; at the same time that the same ownership of
large wealth controls the markets and thereby controls the conditions of life for those who have to resort to the markets to sell
or to buy. In other words, it has come to pass with the change of
circumstances that the rule of Live and Let Live now waits on
the discretion of the owners of large wealth. In fact, those thoughtful men in the eighteenth century who made so much of these
constituent principles of the modern point of view did not con-
template anything like the system of large wealth, large-scale
industry, and large-scale commerce and credit which prevails
today. They did not foresee the new order in industry and business, and the system of rights and obligations which they installed, therefore, made no provision for the new order of things
that has come on since their time.

The new order has brought the machine industry, corporation
finance, big business, and the world market. Under this new order in business and industry, business controls industry. Invested
wealth in large holdings controls the country's industrial system,
directly by ownership of the plant, as in the mechanical industries, or indirectly through the market, as in farming. So that the
population of these civilized countries now falls into two main
classes: those who own wealth invested in large holdings and
who thereby control the conditions of life for the rest; and those

who do not own wealth in sufficiently large holdings, and whose conditions of life are therefore controlled by these others. It is a division, not between those who have something and those who have nothing—as many socialists would be inclined to describe it—but between those who own wealth enough to make it count, and those who do not.

And all the while the scale on which the control of industry and the market is exercised goes on increasing; from which it follows that what was large enough for assured independence yesterday is no longer large enough for tomorrow. Seen from another direction, it is at the same time a division between those who live on free income and those who live by work, —a division between the kept classes and the underlying community from which their keep is drawn. It is sometimes spoken of in this bearing—particularly by certain socialists—as a division between those who do no useful work and those who do; but this would be a hasty generalization, since not a few of those persons who have no assured free income also do no work that is of material use, as e.g., menial servants. But the gravest significance of this cleavage that so runs through the population of the advanced industrial countries lies in the fact that it is a division between the vested interests and the common man. It is a division: between those who control the conditions of work and the rate and volume of output and to whom the net output of industry goes as free income, on the one hand, and those others who have the work to do and to whom a livelihood is allowed by these persons in control, on the other hand. In point of numbers it is a very uneven division, of course.

A vested interest is a legitimate right to get something for nothing, usually a prescriptive right to an income which is secured by controlling the traffic at one point or another. The owners of such a prescriptive right are also spoken of as a vested interest. Such persons make up what are called the kept classes. But the kept classes also comprise many persons who are entitled to a free income on other grounds than their ownership and control of industry or the market, as, e.g., landlords and other persons classed as "gentry," the clergy, the Crown —where there is a Crown—and its agents, civil and military. Contrasted with these classes who make up the vested interests, and who derive an income from the established order of ownership and privilege, is the common man. He is common in the respect that he is not vested with such a prescriptive right to get something for nothing. And he is called common because such is the common lot of men under the new order of business and industry; and such will continue (increasingly) to be the common lot so long as the enlightened principles of secure ownership and self-help handed down from the eighteenth century continue to rule human affairs by help of the new order of industry.

The kept classes, whose free income is secured to them by the legitimate rights of the vested interests, are less numerous than the common man—less numerous by some ninety-five per cent or thereabouts— and less serviceable to the community at large in perhaps the same proportion, so far as regards any conceivable use for any material purpose. In this sense they are uncommon. But it is not usual to speak of the kept classes as the uncommon classes, inasmuch they personally differ from the common run of mankind in no sensible respect. It is more usual to speak of them as "the better classes," because they are in better circumstances and are better able to do as they like. Their place in the economic scheme of the civilized world is to consume the net product of the country's industry over cost, and so prevent a glut of the market.

But this broad distinction between the kept classes and their vested interests on the one side and the common man on the other side is by no means hard and fast. There are many doubtful cases, and a shifting across the line occurs now and again, but the broad distinction is not doubtful for all that. The great distinguishing mark of the common man is that he is helpless within the rules of the game as it is played in the twentieth century under the enlightened principles of the eighteenth century.

There are all degrees of this helplessness that characterizes the common lot. So much so that certain classes, professions, and occupations—such as the clergy, the military, the courts, police, and legal profession—are perhaps to be classed as belonging primarily with the vested interests, although they can scarcely be counted as vested interests in their own right, but rather as outlying and subsidiary vested interests whose tenure is conditioned on their serving the purposes of those principal and self-directing vested interests whose tenure rests immediately on large holdings of invested wealth. The income which goes to these subsidiary or dependent vested interests is of the nature of free income, in so far that it is drawn from the yearly product of the underlying community; but in another sense it is scarcely to be counted as "free" income, in that its continuance depends on the good will of those controlling vested interests whose power rests on the ownership of large invested wealth. Still it will be found that on any test vote these subsidiary or auxiliary vested interests uniformly range themselves with their superiors in the same class, rather than with the common man. By sentiment and habitual outlook they belong with the kept classes, in that they are staunch defenders of that established order of law and custom which secures the great vested interests in power and insures the free income of the kept classes. In any twofold division of the population these are therefore, on the whole, to be ranged on the side of the old order, the vested interests, and the kept classes, both in sentiment and as regards the circumstances which condition their life and comfort.

Beyond these, whose life-interests are, after all, closely bound up with the kept classes, there are other vested interests of a more doubtful and perplexing kind; classes and occupations which would seem to belong with the common lot, but which range themselves at least provisionally with the vested interests and can scarcely be denied standing as such. Such, as an illustrative instance, is the A.F. of L. Not that the constituency of the A.F. of L. can be said to live on free income, and is therefore to be counted in with the kept classes—the only reservation on that head would conceivably be the corps of officials in the A.F. of L., who dominate the policies of that organization and exercise a prescriptive right to dispose of its forces, at the same time that they habitually come in for an income drawn from the underlying organization. The rank and file assuredly are not of the kept classes, nor do they visibly come in for a free income. Yet they stand on the defensive in maintaining a vested interest in the prerogatives and perquisites of their organization. They are apparently moved by a feeling that so long as the established arrangements are maintained they will come in for a little something over and above what would come to them if they were to make common cause with the undistinguished common lot. In other words, they have a vested interest in a narrow margin of preference over and above what goes to the common man. But this narrow margin of net gain over the common lot, this vested right to get a narrow margin of something for nothing, has hitherto been sufficient to shape their sentiments and outlook in such a way as, in effect, to keep them loyal to the large business interests with whom they negotiate for this narrow margin of preference. As is true of the vested interests in business, so in the case of the A.F. of L., the ordinary ways and means of enforcing their claim to a little something over and above is the use of a reasonable sabotage, in the way of restriction, retardation, and unemployment. Yet the constituency of the A.F. of L., taken man for man, is not readily to be distinguished from the common sort so far as regards their conditions of life. The spirit of vested interest which animates them may, in fact, be nothing more to the point than an aimless survival.

Farther along the same line, larger and even more perplexing, is the case of the American farmers, who also are in the habit of ranging themselves, on the whole, with the vested interests rather than with the common man. By sentiment and outlook the farmers are, commonly, steady votaries of that established order which enables the vested interests to do a big business at their expense. Such is the tradition which still binds the farmers, however unequivocally their material circumstances under the new order of business and industry might seem to drive the other way. In the ordinary case the American farmer is now as helpless to control his own conditions of life as the commonest of the common run. He is caught between the vested interests who buy cheap and the vested interests who sell dear, and it is for him to take or leave what is offered, —but ordinarily to take it, on pain of "getting left."

There is still afloat among the rural population a slow-dying tradition of the "Independent Farmer," who is reputed once upon a time to have lived his own life and done his own work, and who was content to let the world wag. But all that has gone by now as completely as the other things that are told in tales which begin with "Once upon a time." It has gone by into the same waste of regrets with the like independence which the country-town retailer is believed to have enjoyed once upon a time. But the country-town retailer, too, still stands stiffly on the vested rights of the trade and of the town; he is by sentiment and habitual outlook a businessman who guides, or would like to guide, his enterprise by the principle of charging what the traffic will bear, of buying cheap and selling dear. He still manages to sell dear, but he does not commonly buy cheap, except what he buys of the farmer, for the massive vested interests in the background now decide for him, in the main, how much his traffic will bear. He is not placed so very differently from the farmer in this respect, except that, being a middleman, he can in some appreciable degree shift the burden to a third party. The third party in the case is the farmer; the massive vested interests who move in the background of the market do not lend themselves to that purpose.

Except for the increasing number of tenant farmers, the American farmers of the large agricultural sections still are owners who cultivate their own ground. They are owners of property, who might be said to have an investment in their own farms, and therefore they fancy that they have a vested interest in the farm and its earning-capacity. They have carried over out of the past and its old order of things a delusion to the effect that they have something to lose. It is quite a natural and rather an engaging delusion, since, barring encumbrances, they are seized of a good and valid title at law, to a very tangible and useful form of property. And by due provision of law and custom they are quite free to use or abuse their holdings in the land, to buy and sell it and its produce altogether at their own pleasure. It is small wonder if the farmers, with the genial traditions of the day before yesterday still running full and free in their sophisticated brains, are given to consider themselves typical holders of a legitimate vested interest of a very substantial kind. In all of which they count without their host; their host, under the new order of business, being those massive vested interests that move obscurely in the background of the market, and whose rule of life it is to buy cheap and sell dear.

In the ordinary case the farmers of the great American farming regions are owners of the land and improvements, except for an increasing proportion of tenant farmers. But it is the farmer-owner

that is commonly had in mind in speaking of the American farmers as a class. Barring encumbrances, these farmer-owners have
a good and valid title to their land and improvements; but their
title remains good only so long as the run of the market for what
they need and for what they have to sell does not take such a
turn that the title will pass by process of liquidation into other
hands, as may always happen. And the run of the market which
conditions the farmer's work and livelihood has now come to
depend on the highly impersonal maneuvers of those massive
interests that move in the background and find a profit in buying
cheap and selling dear. In point of law and custom there is, of
course, nothing to hinder the American farmer from considering
himself to be possessed of a vested interest in his farm and its
working, if that pleases his fancy. The circumstances which decide what he may do with his farm and its equipment, however,
are prescribed for him quite deliberately and quite narrowly by
those other vested interests in the background, which are massive enough to regulate the course of things in business and industry at large. He is caught in the system, and he does not govern the set and motions of the system. So that the question of his
effectual standing as a vested interest becomes a question of fact,
not of preference and genial tradition.

A vested interest is a legitimate right to get something for nothing. The American farmer—say, the ordinary farmer of the grain-
growing Midwest—can be said to be possessed of such a vested
interest if he habitually and securely gets something in the way
of free income above cost, counting as cost the ordinary rate of
wages for work done on the farm plus ordinary returns on the
replacement value of the means of production which he employs.
Now it is notorious that, except for quite exceptional cases, there
are no intangible assets in farming; and intangible assets are the
chief and ordinary indication of free income, that is to say, of
getting something for nothing. Any concern that can claim no
intangible assets, in the way of valuable goodwill, monopoly
rights, or outstanding corporation securities, has no substantial
claim to be rated as a vested interest. What constitutes a valid claim
to standing as a vested interest is the assured customary ability to
get something more in the way of income than a full equivalent for
tangible performance in the way of productive work.

The returns which these farmers are in the habit of getting from their own work and from the work of their household and hired help do not ordinarily include anything that can be called free or unearned income, —unless one should go so far as to declare that income reckoned at ordinary rates on the tangible assets engaged in this industry is to be classed as unearned income, which is not the usual meaning of the expression. It may be that popular opinion on these matters will take such a turn some time that men will come to consider that income which is derived from the use of land and equipment is rightly to be counted as unearned income, because it does not correspond to any tangible performance in the way of productive work on the part of the person to whom it goes. But for the present that is not the popular sense of the matter, and that is not the meaning of the words in popular usage. For the present, at least, reasonable returns on the replacement value of tangible assets are not considered to be unearned income.

It is true, the habits of thought engendered by the machine system in industry and by the mechanically standardized organization of daily life under this new order, as well as by the material sciences, are of such a character as would incline the common man to rate all men and things in terms of tangible performance rather than in terms of legal title and ancient usage. And it may well come to pass, in time, that men will consider any income unearned which exceeds a fair return for tangible performance in the way of productive work on the part of the person to whom the income goes. The mechanistic logic of the new order of industry drives in that direction, and it may well be that the frame of mind engendered by this training in matter-of-fact ways of thinking will presently so shape popular sentiment that all income from property, simply on the basis of ownership, will be disallowed, whether the property is tangible or intangible. All that is a speculative question running into the future. It is to be recognized and taken account of that the immutable principles of law and equity, in matters of ownership and income as well as in other connections, are products of habit, and that habits are always liable to change in response to altered circumstances, and the drift of circumstances is now apparently setting in that direction. But popular sentiment has not yet reached that degree of emancipation from those good old principles of self-help and secure ownership that go to make up the modern (eighteenth-century) point of view in law and custom. The equity of income derived from the use of tangible property may presently become a moot question; but it is not so today, outside of certain classes in the population whom the law and the courts are endeavoring to discourage. It is the business of the law and the courts to discourage any change of insight or opinion.

It appears, therefore, that his conditions of life should throw the American farmer in with the common man who has substantially nothing to lose, beyond what the vested interests of business can always take over at their own discretion and in their own good time. In point of material fact he has ceased to be a self-directing agent, and self-help has for him come substantially to be a make-believe; although, of course, in point of legal formality he still continues to enjoy all the ancient rights and immunities of secure ownership and self-help. Yet it is no less patent a fact of current history that the American farmer continues, on the whole, to stand fast by those principles of self-help and free bargaining which enable the vested interests to play fast and loose with him and all his works. Such is the force of habit and tradition.

The reason, or at least the preconception, by force of which the American farmers have been led, in effect, to side with the vested interests rather than with the common man, comes of the fact that the farmers are not only farmers but also owners of speculative real estate. And it is as speculators in land-values that they find themselves on the side of unearned income. As landowners they aim and confidently hope to get something for nothing in the unearned increase of land-values. But all the while they overlook the fact that the future increase of land-values, on which they pin their hopes, is already discounted in the present price of the land, —except for exceptional and fortuitous cases. As is known to all persons who are at all informed on this topic, farmland holdings in the typical American farming regions are overcapitalized, in the sense that the current market value of these farmlands is considerably greater than the capitalized value of the income to be derived from their current use as farmlands. This excess value of the farmlands is a speculative value due to

discounting the future increased value which these lands are expected to gain with the further growth of population and with
increasing facilities for marketing the farm products of the local-
ity. It is therefore as a land speculator holding his land for a rise,
not as a husbandman cultivating the soil for a livelihood, that the
prairie farmer, e.g., comes in for an excess value and an over-
capitalization of his holdings. All of which has much in common
with the intangible assets of the vested interests, and all of which
persuades the prairie farmer that he is of a class apart from the
common man who has nothing to lose.

But he can come in for this unearned gain only by the eventual sale of his holdings, not in their current use as a means of
production in farming. As a businessman doing a speculative
business in farmlands the American farmer, in a small way, runs
true to form and so is entitled to a modest place among that class
of substantial citizens who get something for nothing by cornering the supply and " sitting tight." And all the while the massive
interests that move obscurely in the background of the market
are increasingly in a position, in their own good time, to disallow the farmer just so much of this still-born gain as they may
dispassionately consider to be convenient for their own ends.
And so the farmer-speculator of the prairie continues to stand
fast by the principles of equity which entitle these vested interests to play fast and loose with him and all his works.

The facts of the case stand somewhat different as regards the
American farmer's gains from his work as a husbandman, or from
the use which he makes of his land and stock in farming. His
returns from his work are notably scant. So much so that it is still
an open question whether, taken one with another, the American
farmer's assets in land and other equipment enable him, one year
with another, to earn more than what would count as ordinary
wages for the labor which these assets enable him to put into his
product. But it is beyond question that the common run of those
American farmers who "work their own land" get at the best a
very modest return for the use of their land and stock, —so scant,
indeed, that if usage admitted such an expression, it would be
fair to say that the farmer, considered as a going concern, should
be credited with an appreciable item of "negative intangible assets," such as habitually to reduce the net average return on his

total active assets appreciably below the ordinary rate of discount. His case, in other words, is the reverse of the typical business concern of the larger sort, which comes in for a net excess over ordinary rates of discount on its tangible assets, and which is thereby enabled to write into its accounts a certain amount of intangible assets, and so come into line as a vested interest. The farmer, too, is caught in the net of the new order; but his occupation does not belong to that new order of business enterprise in which earning-capacity habitually outruns the capitalized value of the underlying physical property.

Evidently the cleavage due to be brought on by the new order in business and industry, between the vested interests and the common man, has not yet fallen into clear lines, at least not in America. The common man does not know himself as such, at least not yet, and the sections of the population which go to make up the common lot as contrasted with the vested interests have not yet learned to make common cause. The American tradition stands in the way. This tradition says that the people of the republic are made up of ungraded masterless men who enjoy all the rights and immunities of self-direction, self-help, free bargaining, and equal opportunity, quite after the fashion that was sketched into the great constituent documents of the eighteenth century.

Much doubt and some discontent is afoot. It is becoming increasingly evident that the facts of everyday life under the new order do not fall in with the inherited principles of law and custom; but the farmers, farm laborers, factory hands, mine workmen, lumber hands, and retail tradesmen have not come to anything like a realization of that new order of economic life which throws them in together on one side of a line of division, on the other side of which stand the vested interests and the kept classes. They have not yet come to realize that all of them together have nothing to lose except such things as the vested interests can quite legally and legitimately deprive them of, with full sanction of law and custom as it runs, so soon and so far as it shall suit the convenience of the vested interests to make such a move. These people of the variegated mass have no safeguard, in fact, against the control of their conditions of life exercised by those massive interests that move obscurely in the background of the market, except such considerations of expediency as may govern the maneuvers of those massive ones who so move obscurely in the background. That is to say, the conditions of life for the variegated mass are determined by what the traffic will bear, according to the calculations of self-help which guide the vested interests, all the while that the farmers, workmen, consumers, the common lot, are still animated with the fancy that they have themselves something to say in these premises.

It is otherwise with the vested interests, on the whole. They take a more perspicuous view of their own case and of the predicament of the common man, the party of the second part. Whereas the variegated mass that makes up the common lot have not hitherto deliberately taken sides together or defined their own attitude toward the established system of law and order and its continuance, and so are neither in the right nor in the wrong as regards this matter, the vested interests and the kept classes, on the other hand, have reached insight and definition of what they need, want, and are entitled to. They have deliberated and chosen their part in the division, partly by interest and partly by ingrained habitual bent, no doubt, —and they are always in the right. They owe their position and the blessings that come of it— free income and social prerogative—to the continued enforcement of these eighteenth-century principles of law and order under conditions created by the twentieth-century state of the industrial arts. Therefore, it is incumbent on them, in point of expediency, to stand strongly for the established order of inalienable eighteenth-century rights; and they are at the same time in the right, in point of law and morals, in so doing, since what is right in law and morals is always a question of settled habit, and settled habit is always a legacy out of the past. To take their own part, therefore, the vested interests and the kept classes have nothing more perplexing to do than simply to follow the leadings of their settled code in all questions of law and order and thereby to fall neatly in with the leading of their own pecuniary advantage, and always and on both counts to keep their poise as safe and sound citizens intelligently abiding by the good old principles of right and honest living which safeguard their vested rights.

The common man is not so fortunate. He cannot effectually take his own part in this difficult conjuncture of circumstances without getting on the wrong side of the established run of law and morals. Unless he is content to go on as the party of the second part in a traffic that is controlled by the massive interests on the footing of what they consider that the traffic will bear, he will find himself in the wrong and may even come in for the comfortless attention of the courts. Whereas if he makes his peace with the established run of law and custom, and so continues to be rated as a good man and true, he will find that his livelihood falls into a dubious and increasingly precarious case. It is not for nothing that he is a common man.

So caught in a quandary, it is small wonder if the common man is somewhat irresponsible and unsteady in his aims and conduct, so far as touches industrial affairs. A pious regard for the received code of right and honest living holds him to a submissive quietism, a make-believe of self-help and fair dealings; whereas the material and pecuniary circumstances that condition his livelihood under this new order drive him to fall back on the underlying rule of Live and Let Live, and to revise the established code of law and custom to such purpose that this underlying rule of life shall be brought into bearing in point of fact as well as in point of legal formality. And the training to which the hard matter-of-fact logic of the machine industry and the mechanical organization of life now subjects him, constantly bends him to a matter-of-fact outlook, to a rating of men and things in terms of tangible performance, and to an ever slighter respect for the traditional principles that have come down from the eighteenth century. The common man is constantly and increasingly exposed to the risk of becoming an undesirable citizen in the eyes of the votaries of law and order. In other words, vested rights to free income are no longer felt to be secure in case the common man should take over the direction of affairs.

Such a vested right to free income, that is to say this legitimate right of the kept classes to their keep at the cost of the underlying community, does not fall in with the lines of that mechanistic outlook and mechanistic logic which is forever gaining ground as the new order of industry goes forward. Such free income, which measures neither the investor's personal contribution to the production of goods nor his necessary consumption while engaged in industry, does not fit in with that mechanistic reckoning that runs in terms of tangible performance, and that grows ever increasingly habitual and convincing with every further habituation to the new order of things in the industrial world. Vested perquisites have no place in the new scheme of things; hence the new scheme is a menace. It is true, the well stabilized principles of the eighteenth century still continue to rate the investor as a producer of goods; but it is equally true that such a rating is palpable nonsense according to the mechanistic calculus of the new order, brought into bearing by the mechanical industry and material science. This may all be an untoward and distasteful turn of circumstances, but there is no gain of tranquillity to be got from ignoring it.

So it comes about that, increasingly, throughout broad classes in these industrial countries there is coming to be visible a lack of respect and affection for the vested interests, whether of business or of privilege; and it rises to the pitch of distrust and plain disallowance among those peoples on whom the preconceptions of the eighteenth century sit more lightly and loosely. It still is all vague and shifty. So much so that the guardians of law and order are still persuaded that they "have the situation in hand." But the popular feeling of incongruity and uselessness in the current run of law and custom under the rule of these timeworn preconceptions is visibly gaining ground and gathering consistency, even in so well ordered a republic as America. A cleavage of sentiment is beginning to run between the vested interests and the variegated mass of the common lot; and increasingly the common man is growing apathetic, or even impervious, to appeals grounded on these timeworn preconceptions of equity and good usage.

The fact of such a cleavage, as well as the existence of any ground for it, is painstakingly denied by the spokesmen of the vested interests; and in support of that comfortable delusion they will cite the exemplary fashion in which certain monopolistic labor organizations "stand pat." It is true, such a quasi-vested interest of the A.F. of L., which unbidden assumes to speak for the common man, can doubtless be counted on to "stand pat" on that system of imponderables in which its vested perquisites reside. So also the kept classes, and their stewards among the keepers of law and custom, are inflexibly content to let well enough alone. They can be counted on to see nothing more to the point than a stupidly subversive rapacity in that loosening of the bonds of convention that so makes light of the sacred rights of vested interest. Interested motives may count for something on both sides, but it is also true that the kept classes and the businesslike managers of the vested interests, whose place in the economy of nature it is to make money by conforming to the received law and custom, have not in the same degree undergone the shattering discipline of the New Order. They are, therefore, still to be found standing blamelessly on the stable principles of the Modern Point of View.

But a large fraction of the people in the industrial countries is visibly growing uneasy under these principles as they work out under existing circumstances. So, e.g., it is evident that the common man within the United Kingdom, in so far as the Labor Party is his accredited spokesman, is increasingly restive under the state of "things as they are," and it is scarcely less evident that he finds his abiding grievance in the Vested Interests and that system of law and custom which cherishes them. And these men, as well as their like in other countries, are still in an unsettled state of advance to positions more definitely at variance with the received law and custom. In some instances, and indeed in more or less massive formation, this movement of dissent has already reached the limit of tolerance and has found itself sharply checked by the constituted keepers of law and custom.

It is perhaps not unwarranted to count the I.W.W. as such a vanguard of dissent, in spite of the slight consistency and the exuberance of its movements. After all, these and their like, here and in other countries are an element of appreciable weight in the population. They are also increasingly numerous, in spite of well-conceived repressive measures, and they appear to grow increasingly sure. And it will not do to lose sight of the presumption that, while they may be gravely in the wrong, they are likely not to be far out of touch with the undistinguished mass of the common sort who still continue to live within the law. It should seem likely that the peculiar moral and intellectual bent which marks them as "undesirable citizens" will, all the while, be found to run closer to that of the common man than the corresponding bent of the law-abiding beneficiaries under the existing system.

Vaguely, perhaps, and with a picturesque irresponsibility, these and their like are talking and thinking at cross-purposes with the principles of free bargain and self-help. There is reason to believe that to their own thinking, when cast in the terms in which they conceive these things, their notions of reasonable human intercourse are not equally fantastic and inconclusive. So, there is the dread word, Syndicalism, which is quite properly unintelligible to the kept classes and the adepts of corporation finance, and which has no definable meaning within the constituent principles of the eighteenth century. But the notion of it seems to come easy, by mere lapse of habit, to these others in whom the discipline of the New Order has begun to displace the preconceptions of the eighteenth century.

Then there are, in this country, the agrarian syndicalists, in the shape of the Nonpartisan League, — large, loose, animated, and untidy, but sure of itself in its settled disallowance of the Vested Interests, and fast passing the limit of tolerance in its inattention to the timeworn principles of equity. How serious is the moral dereliction and the subversive stupidity of these agrarian syndicalists, in the eyes of those who still hold fast to the eighteenth century, may be gathered from the animation of the business community, the commercial clubs, the Rotarians, and the traveling salesmen, in any place where the League raises its untidy head. And as if advisedly to complete the case, these agrarians, as well as their running mates in the industrial centers and along the open road, are found to be slack in respect of their national spirit. So, at least, it is said by those who are interested to know.

It is not that these and their like are ready with "a satisfactory constructive program," such as the people of the uplift require to be shown before they will believe that things are due to change. It is something of the simpler and cruder sort, such as history is full of, to the effect that whenever and so far as the timeworn rules no longer fit the new material circumstances they presently fail to carry conviction as they once did. Such wear and tear of institutions is unavoidable where circumstances change; and it is through the altered personal equation of those elements of the population which are most directly exposed to the changing circumstances that the wear and tear of institutions may be expected to take effect. To these untidy creatures of the New Order common honesty appears to mean vaguely something else, perhaps something more exacting, than what was "nominated in the bond" at the time when the free bargain and self-help were written into the moral constitution of Christendom by the handicraft industry and the petty trade. And why should it not?

For Product Safety Concerns and Information please contact our EU
representative GPSR@taylorandfrancis.com
Taylor & Francis Verlag GmbH, Kaufingerstraße 24, 80331 München, Germany

www.ingramcontent.com/pod-product-compliance
Ingram Content Group UK Ltd.
Pitfield, Milton Keynes, MK11 3LW, UK
UKHW020945180425
457613UK00019B/525